MW00935073

THE DEAD END KIDS OF PORT RICHMOND, PHILADELPHIA: A MEMOIR

By

Ed Chrzanowski

God willing, hope to see
you at our 60 th.
Ed Chrzanowski '47
(Compliments of
John Collins, Esq. '47)

© 2002 by Ed Chrzanowski. All rights reserved.

No part of this book may be reproduced, restored in a
retrieval system, or transmitted by means, electronic,
mechanical, photocopying, recording, or otherwise, without
written consent from the author.

ISBN: 1-4033-0643-5 (e-book)
ISBN: 1-4033-0644-3 (Paperback)

This book is printed on acid free paper.

1st Books - rev. 06/27/02

Prologue

Nature is kind to older people who decide to write their memoirs late in life. I'm 72, and my memory of my distant past is sharpening, while my memory of my immediate past is dimming, ideal for memoir writing. Still, my memory of my immediate past has not dimmed so much that I don't know what's been happening lately. I live in the small city of Lockport, New York, population 20,000, about 20 miles south of Buffalo and about 20 miles west of Niagara Falls. After I left the Roman Catholic priesthood in 1977, I moved here because the woman I loved lived here. Eventually, I married her three years later.

I'm Polish, of course. Both my parents, who hardly spoke any English, were born in Poland. But I'm often taken to be Irish. I've been compared to former House Speaker Tip O'Neill, to football commentator John Madden, to Senator Ted Kennedy, to actor Charles Laughton, in his younger days, I hope. My wife, Shirley Mahar, German-Irish, is a few years younger. She was a Roman Catholic nun for 19 years before she left in 1973. She is beautiful, exteriorly and interiorly. I met her in Toledo, Ohio, in 1975. A priest friend invited me to join him, his sister, and her friend Shirley to dinner. That's how it all started. Innocently enough.

In the priesthood I taught high school and did parish work on weekends. I taught in Philadelphia, my hometown, as a seminarian for two years and for two years after I was ordained a priest in 1957. I taught in Niagara Falls, New York, and in Toledo, Ohio. Since leaving the priesthood, I have sold encyclopedias, energy-saving devices, accident and health insurance, AAA memberships, real estate, and probably a few other things I have forgotten. I taught part-time English in various high schools and colleges. I wrote part-time for two daily newspapers. I taught college English and philosophy part-time in several state prisons. I worked full-time for nine years as a college counselor and as a teacher at Attica Correctional Facility. Now I do part-time legal research for the *Buffalo Law Journal*, a twice-weekly publication, and I write resumes from home.

1

But now I would like to focus, not exclusively, and not strictly chronologically, on my first 18 years growing up in Philadelphia before I left for the seminary in 1947. I grew up in a section of Northeast Philadelphia called Port Richmond, so called because the eastern end of our section of the city was bordered by the Delaware River where there was a small port called Port Richmond. On the other side of the river is the state of New Jersey.

My earliest recollection is of lying on my mother's bosom my arms wrapped around her neck, my cheek against her cheek, her arms securely wrapped around my little body. My eyes were looking beyond my mother at a pretty scene. It was the back kitchen window looking out into our small backyard garden, overgrown with all kinds of plants and flowers and bushes. My mother, sitting on an old leather rocking chair in our kitchen, was rocking me to sleep, purring a Polish lullaby about *kotki* (kittens). Many years later this scene came back to me when a Fr. Jim Bacik, a budding Notre Dame University theologian, asked his audience in Toledo to try to remember their very first experience of life. Fr. Bacik said the first remembrance of life often determines one's personality. Maybe that's why I'm so calm, pleasant, gentle, so laid back (I've been called a Gentle Giant on numerous occasions.). In fact, a priest-friend said if I were anymore laid back, I'd be going backwards. All my remembrances of my mother mirror that earliest one: calm, peaceful, reassuring.

My next earliest recollection of life must have been at least months later as a toddler because I was able to wield a foot-long ruler. I was lying on a sofa without a back to it in our kitchen. With this ruler I was beating an imaginary object hidden behind the pillows. I missed the pillows and hit the wall and down came plaster from the wall, leaving a gaping hole. Terrified of my father, who would soon be home from work, I stacked pillows against the hole. It worked; at least I wasn't punished. Either my mother covered for me or my father exhibited a rare case of leniency. That's my earliest recollection of my father, basically, one of fear.

My earliest recollection of my three older brothers was riding one of them, on all fours on the living room rug, as a bucking horse. After he threw me off, he would engage me in a fight. He would slap me lightly with his open hands, and I would punch him as hard as I could with my closed fists. Someone, I think it was Walt, was letting out his frustrations one day and hitting me back hard enough to hurt. So I quickly stopped playing this game of fisticuffs with my older brothers.

I remember another early episode. My next oldest brother, Walt, placed me on a borrowed bicycle to take me for a ride. He told me very distinctly to hold on to the handle bars tightly and to be careful not to place my foot in the spokes of the front wheel, which I promptly did when he turned the front wheel sharply to the left. I bent a few of the spokes, for which I was scolded by Walt, and I tore up my shoe, for which I was roundly scolded by my mother. Nobody seemed to care that my toes were badly bruised.

2

My parents must have been surprised when my mother became pregnant with me, for there was an interval of eight years between me and my next oldest brother, Walt. They were probably disappointed, too, because I was born during the Depression: July 5, 1929. And my mother must have been doubly disappointed because I was a boy: her fourth straight son. How she must have wanted another feminine presence in the home, which I sensed she did many times as I was growing up. And later in college my mother's loneliness and desperation struck me vividly when I read one of Sherwood Anderson's short stories. It dealt with a woman in an insensitive all-male household. I identified my mother with that woman in the story: both trapped in an all-male existence, bereft of any femininity, any sensitivity. The few times I saw my mother when she allowed her femininity to show was when she took care of her flowers and bushes in her 6-by-8 foot garden in the backyard, where not a single foot of soil was without growth of some kind. She would be humming with a smile on her face, watering this flower, pruning that bush, lost in her own little world, until it was time to come in to take care of another household chore. Another time she would exhibit her femininity was when she prepared for Sunday Mass. She would put on her Sunday dress on her short, ample body; take the hat from the hatbox above the closet in the middle upstairs room and in front of a mirror in the living room, place the hat on her head at the right angle. She would try this angle, that angle until she got it right, all absorbed in her appearance, Sunday morning, the only time she dressed up and must have felt like a woman.

My brothers and father reached the height of insensitivity, I thought, even at a young age, when my mother received her American citizenship. I was 14 years old, eager to go outside after supper and play. One evening my mother pleaded with me—actually pleaded with me—to stay home and to tutor her in the questions and answers she had to learn for her citizenship test. Reluctantly, I complied. Her pleadings actually touched me, a selfish 14-year-old. Every evening for about a month, Mom and I would sit down at the dinner table and I would quiz her.

"When and by whom was the United States of America discovered?"

And I would answer for her, "Christopher Columbus in 1492."

I would repeat this question and answer a dozen times or so before my mother memorized the answer and could give it back to me in very broken English.

"Who was the first president of the United States?"

"George Washington."

"What are the three branches and their functions of the United States government?"

"The executive, to execute the laws; the legislative, to make the laws, and the judiciary, to enforce the laws."

"What form of legislature does the United States government have?"

"Bicameral."

And so on and so on. I'm sure my mother did not understand the meaning of many of these questions and answers, nor did I. It was an exercise in brute memory.

Finally, the big day came to take the test and to be sworn in as an American citizen if she passed. I'm sure it was a day my mother looked forward to for a long time, actually 29 years since her arrival in this country in 1914. Both of us, dressed in our Sunday best, took the 60 trolley car at Thompson and Allegheny to Kensington and Allegheny Avenues. We took the elevated and subway train to 4th & Market Streets and walked to Chestnut Street to the United States Custom House building. My mother passed the test, and when she was sworn in as a citizen of the United States with dozens of others, after nearly 30 years of living in this country, we both cried. My mother beamed with pride as we walked down the Custom House steps. According to her citizenship papers, it was March 26, 1943, a most auspicious day for my mother.

Instead of getting off at Thompson Street, we took the 60 trolley car to the next stop, to the end of the line, to the car barn at Richmond Street. My mother was going to treat herself and me to dinner at a restaurant. I was surprised but glad. We went to the only half-decent restaurant in Port Richmond at the time, Pep's Restaurant, operated by Greeks. I ordered for both of us, the special of the day: ground steak, mashed potatoes, smothered in a mushroom gravy, and peas. It was the first time either of us had dinner in a restaurant.

We walked home to a sullen group of males because their dinner wasn't ready on time. They seemed to understand and forgave Mom because nobody complained. Nor did anybody congratulate her, hug her, and kiss her, for probably her proudest achievement. I think they wanted to but didn't know how. Mom changed her clothes and prepared dinner.

Mom, Pop, and me on a Sunday afternoon visit to the
Blusiewicz farm. Around 1932.

3

Although my parents were probably surprised and my mother was disappointed by my birth, I almost didn't make it into this world. It was many years later when I was 25 years old and about to be ordained a priest that I thought it was time for my mother to stop addressing me publicly, in heavily-Polish-accented English, as "my baby." "The public will soon be calling me 'Father,' Mom," I argued, "and you still call me 'baby.'" She never called me "baby" again.

My mother explained why I was her special baby and at the same time answered a question that long perplexed me: how did I get that slight but noticeable depression on the right side of my forehead? My mother said the family doctor delivering me at home told my father my head was too large: it was either my mother or me. My father with three young boys to raise opted to save my mother's life. But using forceps and depressing my head slightly with them, the doctor managed to squeeze me out of my mother's womb.

In my own limited way, I tried at times to take the place of the daughter my mother never had. I would clear the table, wipe off the crumbs, often wiping more on to the floor, dry (not wash) the dishes, iron the handkerchiefs (converted five-pound sugar bags). I would run her errands to Radzikowski's corner butcher shop and grocery store in one direction at the end of the block to Madison Street and to Majeski's delicatessen and Maxie Shapiro's produce store in the other direction to Allegheny Avenue.

I never minded much going to Radzikowskis, a Ma' and Pa' store if there ever was one, because I enjoyed bounding over the white marble steps of the row houses. I would leave the house, turn left, jump from ours and our next-door neighbor's step, the Senskes, a very nice elderly German couple with a grown son and daughter, take a few steps more and bound onto Tom Mix and Dillo's steps, with their alcoholic mother and prostitute sister, Eleanor, who plied her trade in downtown Philadelphia. Eleanor might have been a lovely girl in her youth but she was then, even in my young eyes, a thin, emaciated, physically ugly woman, old beyond her years, who couldn't ply her trade anymore. She returned home and now sat on the front steps all day long, smoking cigarettes, drinking beer with her mother. She died soon afterwards, before her mother.

Then onto and over Chubby and Jimmy DiPersio's and their divorcee (scandalous) mother's home. Jimmy DiPersio was one of the few guys without a nickname, unless you can call DiPersio a nickname. He was about five years older than I. Handsome with dark curly hair, clear skin, a fast, smooth talker. Everything about him was fast; when he spoke you felt he was trying to con you. I heard, years later, he did rise to the top, in our estimation. He bought a nightclub in downtown Philadelphia, and I heard he died an early death. (I hope it was a natural death.)

We called DiPersio's younger brother, Eugene, Chubby ever since they moved into the neighborhood because he was chubby. It was difficult for Chubby to be accepted by us; he wasn't Polish, he went to a public school, he was chubby, not very athletic, and he never fought back when he was called a sissy. For the next few years we didn't see Chubby. He seemed to have vanished. What he did was change his circle of friends. He began to circulate with the Putso Gang, an Italian gang from the Cambria-Somerset area, about a half dozen blocks south of Allegheny Avenue where we Poles hung out. He was getting a reputation as a tough guy, a street brawler, which was hard to believe. But when I saw him, I believed it. I saw him walking home one afternoon, about five inches taller, muscular, with no baby fat. His hair was still blond, fashioned into a pompadour in front and combed in the back into a DA (duck's ass), wearing a black leather jacket with peg pants (pants tight at the ankles and voluminous at the knees) with a long, gold key chain extending from his belt to his knee and up again to his right pocket. Accompanied by an entourage, he walked with a swagger, a cigarette hanging out of his mouth. His voice deepened over the years; he spoke with a snarl;

his face was expressionless; his look was penetrating, even menacing.

Chubby somehow transformed himself from a sissy into a leader of the Putso Gang. The roles were reversed; we now were the sissies. And it was Chubby a few months later who instigated a gang war one summer evening between the Putsos (the Italian gang) and the K&A (Kensington and Allegheny Avenues) gang (the Irish Gang) at Cohocksink Playground at Gaul and Ann Streets. We of the Allegheny Gang, if you could call us that, got wind of the rumble. We rushed down to Aramingo and Allegheny Avenues just as the K&A gang arrived from the other direction from Kensington and Allegheny, carrying baseball bats, pipes, chains and possibly hidden weapons. (The gang scene from "West Side Story" evoked memories of this scene.) The crowd, the excitement, the hysteria swept me along. More and more kids joined the crowd as we marched unevenly up wide, cobblestoned Aramingo Avenue, with people straining their necks from their front porches, wondering what was going on. With every step I became more terrified. I saw guys next to me with weapons and I was weaponless, not that I would know how to use one if I had one. I wanted to stop marching, get out of the rumble (I didn't even know what it was about.) and run home, but I would be called chicken Once you were in it, you had to stay in it, so I stayed. As we approached the intersection of Aramingo and Indiana Streets just a few blocks before Cohocksink Playground, I was never so happy to see the pulsating red lights of four police cars. A policeman with a bullhorn got out of his car and told us to turn around and go home. The rumble was over. And we did. And we were glad. After I entered the seminary, I and everybody else lost track of Chubby. I would be surprised if he were still alive.

4

It was about this time when we were 15 or 16 years old in the mid '40s that a strange and powerful transformation was taking place in the neighborhood. Everybody, not only Chubby (Maybe they were following his example.), wanted to be known as a fighter, as a street-brawler, as a tough guy. That was the topic of conversation every evening at Harry's Ice Cream Parlor at Salmon and Allegheny Avenue: who beat whom yesterday. It seemed as if there were fistfights every other night and occasional mob fights. There was the story of Sammy, the 300-pound tackle who tried out for the Eagles, and who beat up five guys at the Polish American Dance one Saturday night. (This was not a story. I witnessed it.) There was the story of Huntzy beating up Dillo for making a pass at his girl. Everybody was fighting, beating up somebody.

Out of all this barbaric behavior, the most unlikely candidate emerged as the most barbaric: nice, cheerful, friendly, good-natured Corpo. He suddenly got the reputation of being the toughest kid in the neighborhood with a half-dozen, maybe a dozen notches in his belt. He had a fight a week, at least. Corpo was of average size, about 5'9", about 160 pounds, muscularly built, with big knuckled hands. He was fast on his feet and fast with his fists. He seemed to delight in his newfound reputation as the tough guy in the neighborhood.

Corpo and I were close friends for about five years. He found for me the pinsetting job at the Bowlerdome and later the busboy job at the Bellevue Court Tavern. He had me over his home to meet his sweet mother and lovely family. He was attending Northeast Catholic High School with me.

One evening a bunch of us were hanging out in front of Furtek's at the corner of Mercer and Allegheny. Out of the blue with no provocation, Corpo walked up to me, jabbed me hard in the shoulder blade, put up his fists and said, "C'mon, Wimp, you want to fight?" Startled, I said, "I don't want to fight, Corp."

Jabbing me a few times harder, pushing me back on my heels, he repeated, "C'mon, Wimp, put up your dukes. Let's fight." I was utterly humiliated in front of my friends. "C'mon, Wimp, what are you, chicken? Let's fight." With head bowed, I whispered, "I don't want to fight." I was chicken. Corpo walked away, disgusted, disappointed. I suppose he wanted to add another notch to his belt that night.

I was and am chicken when it comes to fighting. Even though I was surrounded by this fistfight milieu for a number of years, I never had a serious fistfight in my life. It wasn't so much the *fear* of being beaten, of having my front teeth knocked out or my nose broken (which were considerations, I admit) but the *humiliation* of being beaten that made me a chicken. How would I face the gang if I lost a fight? How would I face the guy I lost the fight to?

Not ever having a fistfight weighed on me. I didn't want to go through my youth without experiencing a fistfight. One evening, soon after this fiasco with Corpo, Eddie Labus and I were alone in front of Furtek's. There was no chance of humiliation if I lost; there was nobody there but Labo and me. This was the opportunity I was looking for, so I began to goad Eddie Labus into a fight, just the way Corpo did to me. "C'mon, Labo, let's go to Furtek's garage and fight. C'mon, are you yellow? Are you chicken?" Labo was actually a year older than I, heavier and huskier. Surprisingly, he was reluctant to fight, but he agreed. We actually weren't mad at each other; we had nothing to fight about, but we went to fight because it seemed everybody was doing it. We went to Furtek's driveway. It was winter, it was cold. Labo wore a heavy leather jacket. Whenever we got close enough to each other to hit each other in the face, Labo would turn his back to me and I would pummel his back like a punching bag. We did this for about 15 minutes. After I was exhausted and he was bored, we called it a draw and shook hands. That was my one and only fistfight, if you want to call it that.

Fistfighting was a part of our culture, our millieu as we were growing up. We delighted in hearing about fistfights and we took special delight in witnessing a fistfight firsthand. I witnessed several brutal fistfights. One took place right outside our home. It seemed Slim Ochlak, a tall, thin 40-year old man with a mean disposition, for some flip remark, slapped across the face little Johnny Kijack, the only child, the apple of Mike Kijack's eye, who could also have been nicknamed Slim and who drove a truck for the Independent Meat Rendering Co. that stunk up the neighborhood about every other day during the summer months. Mike was looking all over the neighborhood for Slim and found him playing cards on Mercer Street. Slim was much younger than the balding, bow-legged Mike Kijack, but Mike, as we watched in secret delight, gave Slim a terrible thrashing and would have inflicted serious harm to him if the crowd did not intervene and pull Mike off the bloodied and badly beaten Slim. The cheering crowd suddenly turned silent, probably embarrassed by the secret delight we took in Slim's battered face. That's what, I think, paternal rage can do to a person and that's how crowds react to violence.

I, along with hundreds of others, witnessed another bloody fight at the nearby Allegheny Park. It really wasn't a fight but a bloody beating of a brother. Hank Borowski, a short, squat muscular man in his 40s who lived with his wife on Madison Street, adjacent to the park, found out that his younger brother Matt, who lived with them, was having an affair with his wife for the past few months. Like Mike Kijack, Hank, too, went looking for his adversary, his younger brother this time, and found him sitting unsuspectingly at a park bench near the fountain at the center of the park, where a crowd was sitting and where we were shooting marbles nearby. Suddenly, Matt let out a yell as his older brother hit him, while still sitting, flush in the face with his fist and grabbed him by the top of his hair with his left hand and began dragging him across the park, pummeling him with his right hand in the face every two or three steps towards their home, probably to confront the wife. All the while, Hank is cursing and accusing his younger brother and Matt is cowering, trying to protect his face, begging for mercy, declaring his innocence. Now the crowd grew to what seemed like hundreds of people, all cheering Hank, urging him to beat his brother more, until he reached his home, threw his brother in and shut the door behind them. The spectators returned to their park benches to savor a little bit more what they had just witnessed, and we returned to our game of marbles, still amazed and a bit shaken at what we had just witnessed.

Human nature takes pleasure in witnessing violence, it seems, whether it be on the football field, or in the boxing ring, or when one brother is crunching his fist into the face of his younger brother at the park on a sunny, Saturday afternoon.

My brother Joe was involved in at least one fistfight. I was seven or eight years old at the time. One evening as I was preparing for bed, Joe burst into the house—bleeding profusely from the nose, crying, sobbing uncontrollably. Through sobs he explained that he had a fight with Frank Olejnicz, a neighbor, outside the Royal Café across the street on Allegheny Avenue. Joe went upstairs tore off his bloodied shirt, put his head and face under the faucet in the bathtub for a few minutes. (We did not have a sink.) He washed himself of the blood, sobered up a bit, stopped crying, put on a clean shirt and went back to the Royal Café to get even with Frank. I wanted badly to go with him and watch, but my mother wouldn't let me (Pop was working 4 to 12 that week), so we watched as best we could from a distance from our front doorstep. Soon after Joe entered the saloon, out he came with Frank and the entire bar behind them. They began fighting again. This time Joe was soberer and Frank must have been drunker, probably drinking boilermakers (shot and a beer chaser) to celebrate his victory while Joe was washing and sobering up. We could see them sparring, just jabbing at each other. Joe, a southpaw, kept putting his right fist into the smaller but huskier Frank's face. They would clinch and Joe would hit Frank a couple in the stomach. As they broke the clinch he would hit Frank with a lefthander to the face. By this time, Frank, bleeding from the nose, had enough and conceded victory. Joe and Frank and the crowd went back into the Royal and Joe and Frank probably bought each other a drink.

5

The next step to bound over was the Kolaks', with their six attractive daughters and one son, Sammy. They were rumored to be Polish Gypsies because there were so many of them, because of their dark complexion and because they did not belong to the church.

Sammy, so called, I presume, because of his complexion, was one of the gang. He was good looking, like his sisters, but in a masculine way, until he had an accident when he was twelve. While playing at the cinder yard at Aramingo and Venango, we jumped on a huge rusted pipe situated on a slope and began to roll it, much like log rollers we saw in the movies, toward where the other pipes were. Just as the pipe we were rolling was gaining momentum and approaching the other pipes, Sammy slipped off and fell forward. His face was crushed between two pipes. He survived but he was left with a deep scar that ran across his face from the middle of his cheek to his forehead across his right eye.

Sammy and his six sisters somehow all lived in a two-bedroom home with an outhouse in the backyard. The front room, what would be the parlor of the house, was where Mr. Kolak, who worked in a plant somewhere, moonlighted repairing watches. Almost every night we could see him through his front window bent over with a jeweler's loupe in his right eye, with tweezers in one hand and a watch in the other, and a goose necked lamp shining on the work before him. He was a frightening figure to us young ones looking up at him in the dark. The rumor of his mysterious ancestry only added to the fright.

The Kolak girls were rumored to be morally loose, probably because they were good looking and well endowed and they didn't go to church. I never experienced or witnessed any of that looseness in all my years, although it was not for want of trying. All we ever did was play "Spin the Bottle" with an empty Harbison or Supplee milk bottle as a pointer, or we played Post Office with the Kolak girls. All I remember is a lot of innocent, embarrassed kissing in the dark. But I did experience some of that looseness—much later.

On the Kolaks' pavement in front of their house was the lone city gaslight of the street. Every evening at dusk, the gaslighter would come with his ladder to light the gaslight and because that was the one place on the block that was lit, we would linger and congregate there. Having the six Kolak girls nearby might have been another inducement. And we would shinny up that rather thick iron post to the crossbar near the top. We shinnied up that pole almost nightly, sometimes several times a night because I, at least, enjoyed a nice, pleasant feeling in the lower part of my body when I did so. I never mentioned this feeling to anyone and no one ever mentioned it to me. I think we instinctively figured it was an unmentionable topic. I guess it was the beginning of puberty at a very early age—maybe ten, eleven, twelve.

The prettiest of the Kolak girls, I thought, was Wanda, about five years older than me. She was voluptuous, foul-mouthed, loud, argumentative, a busybody, with a pretty face, a great body and a heart of gold. During World War II she married a marine from the Midwest, lived with him and his family on a farm for a few years, had three children. She became tired of farm life, apparently, and resettled back to Mercer Street about five houses from where she grew up. I heard that marriage didn't change her much, at least that's what I heard from my brother Stan, who moved into the family's house with his five young children after my mother died. I was away in the priesthood. Walt and Joe married and moved away, Joe a few blocks away to Edgemont Street and Walt across the river to Cherry Hill, New Jersey.

Every summer after my mother died, I would spend a few days at the home of my brother Joe and his wife Jean. One evening I walked over to visit with Stan and the kids. By this time, his wife had left him and the kids for another man. Stan was glad to see me. It was clear he had a few beers already but he ran out of the house to Bosak's Bar on Allegheny and Almond St, just a block from Mercer Street, to get two more quarts of Ortlieb's beer, Philadelphia's finest and cheapest. Between beers and amidst the confusion and turmoil of the five kids running around the house, I tried to counsel Stan: "Why do you drink so much beer? You have to take care of these five kids." He answered: "It's cheaper than tranquilizers and it tastes better." I counseled no further.

As I left Stan's home to return to Joe's, Wanda was sitting on her front step with a bottle of Ortlieb's in hand. "Do you want to come in and have a beer, Wimpy?" I accepted her invitation with some misgivings. I just didn't trust the sound of her voice; it was too lyrical, too tempting, too enticing. In the darkened living room was her husband, Ron, sleeping. "He had one too many beers," Wanda said. She led me through the small darkened home to the back kitchen, turned on a single small wattage bulb lamp, hanging over a small circular kitchen table with a red checkered plastic table cover, and turned on a small revolving fan above the refrigerator. She poured me an Ortliebs and freshened up hers and we began to reminisce. She poured me and herself another as we continued to reminisce about her brother Sammy who died a few years earlier and who was a childhood friend of mine, about her sisters, about the neighbors, about my brothers, especially Stan whom she was fond of and whom she was trying to help bring up his five children. She opened another quart of Ortliebs and poured us both another glass and began to talk of religion, how she didn't believe in the Roman Catholic Church, how it was a waste for priests not to be able to marry. She asked how I was coping with my celibacy and asked if I wanted to do something about it. I was taken aback by the question. I didn't respond. I pretended I didn't understand.

Dressed in a low cut, short, loose, flouncy, summer dress with no bra, no stockings, no shoes, (and possibly no panties; I couldn't see), she began to talk admiringly of her past good looks and figure, how all the guys were chasing after her when she was younger and in her prime. She then stood up and moved towards me and invited me to evaluate her present good looks and figure. She grabbed the back of her dress and pulled it tightly around her body, revealing the contours of her slightly sagging breasts, and revealing a deep decolletage. She then placed her right barefoot on my chair between my legs in my crotch and said, "I put a little weight on, Wimp, but these are still pretty nice, aren't they?" as she slowly slid her dress up over her knee, up and up her thigh, and turned her leg one way and the other, with her eyes fastened on me and with a sexy smile on her lips, saying nothing, waiting for me to make a move. I think I might have made a move, vow of chastity or no vow of chastity, celibacy or no celibacy, priesthood or no priesthood, if it weren't for that uneven, hesitant snore emanating from the living room, a scant twenty feet away.

I think Wanda tried to seduce me as a favor to me, or maybe she would have considered it a conquest to seduce a priest. I don't know. At any rate, I said, "Thanks for the beer, Wandz. It was nice talking to you. I've got to go. See you later," and I walked out with some difficulty. It wasn't just the beer.

Since then over the years, I spoke with Wanda often but I was never invited into her home again. She continued to be a good friend and support to my brother Stan and later to his daughter Lucy, who moved in the home after Stan died. When visiting Lucy a few years ago, I heard Wanda was dying after a long illness. I went to the hospital to visit her. She burst into tears when I entered the room. As I leaned over to kiss her on the cheek, she whispered, "Thanks for coming, Wimp." She died the next day.

Then came the Murawski home, located about half way up the 150-yard Mercer Street block, friends of my parents and who stopped in our home on occasion. Mrs. Murawska, despite her 50 years of age or so, was known as a hussy to the neighbors on the block. I recall walking on the opposite side of the street and something caught my eye. I saw her in her bra and panties looking out the front upstairs window. Her first reaction was to cover herself with her arms but then she stopped and threw out her bust as if to say, "Here, Edziu, take a good look." It was at this time she was trying to seduce poor Mr. Furtek, whose truck garage and office were directly across from the Murawskis. (Maybe she expected to see Mr. Furtek when I appeared.) She would come out of her home; he would come out of his office, and they exchanged pleasantries and furtive glances all day long. They behaved like two smitten teenagers, at least Mr. Furtek did. It was obvious to all the neighbors, even to me a 10-12-year-old, that something was going on, and it soon became obvious to Mrs. Furtek, who put a stop to it before something materialized.

6

Mr. Furtek must have been a remarkable man in his day. He was my father's age, a slight man who couldn't speak any English. Yet, he must have been close to a millionaire back then. He owned practically one side of Mercer Street from Madison Street to Allegheny Avenue, at least the length and width of a football field. His empire consisted of a three-story brick building that he rented out to about a dozen truck owners and where he and his only son Joe repaired trucks and cars. He had three rows of garages, totaling about 50 spaces, he rented to neighboring car owners. He had a huge home that contained a dry goods store on the first floor, facing Allegheny Avenue, that Mrs. Furtek operated. On the second floor above the dry goods store, he had a beauty parlor that his daughter Bernadette operated.

Mr. Furtek kept up his property assiduously. All his 50 individual garages were painted a deep green every other year. His garages had six small panes of glass on each of the two doors that swung open. Whenever a pane was broken, usually by us kids, by an errant throw of a ball, a stone, or an errant, or not so errant, BB shot, the broken pane was replaced by the next day. I noticed, however, when I came home from the seminary that Mr. Furtek probably figured it was too much trouble or self-defeating to replace the window with a window that would only be broken again, so he replaced the small broken window with a piece of metal. Today, there is not a single windowpane, only tin plates. Before I was born, a lumberyard stood on the property. The lumberyard moved. Mr. Furtek bought the land and built his "empire" on it. Where did he get the money to build all this? Some say he made his fortune from moonshining during the prohibition. What is the status of this "empire" today? Terrible. Mr. and Mrs. Furtek died while I was in the seminary. Their only son Joe went over to Poland to find a wife. He came back with a wife, who, since Joe's death, owns all the property and is allowing it to deteriorate badly. The big truck garage is vacant; the automobile garages are vacant, boarded up with graffiti-covered boards; (Most of the garages were too small to use for today's bigger cars.) the dry goods store is vacant; the beauty parlor, vacant. The driveway, where we used to play cards, to fight, is now a hangout for druggies, according to my niece Lucy. The fence around the small yard to the Furtek house is about to collapse. The windows of the once well kept home are dirty, curtainless, shades drawn. Joe's widow, now in her late seventies or early eighties, lives alone, practically a recluse. What's going to happen to all this property when she dies? I wonder.

The Furtek property played a big part in our youth. The first row of garages faced Mercer Street. To get to the other two rows you had to turn into a driveway. It was this driveway that was our boxing ring, our hideaway from the cops when we played cards there, our place to play a combination tennis and ping pong game by using the palm of our hands as racquets to hit a tennis or pimple ball to each other over a crack in the driveway. Whenever a fistfight was to take place, the

Ed Chrzanowski

two fighters would walk to Furtek's, take off their jackets and meet under a bright light, with two rows of garages serving as two ropes and with onlookers forming the remaining two ropes of an almost ideal boxing ring. The fight would commence, and whoever gave up first was the loser. Usually, it took a display of some blood for somebody to quit.

7

This is where my brother Stan fought many a fight and where he earned the nick-name of Tiger for his ferocity. The majority of his fights, I understand, were against Joe "Bedbugs" Bednarek, now in his 80s, still alive and well, a retired insurance and real estate broker, and a former bank president.

Stan's success as a street fighter prompted him to pursue a career as a professional boxer. I recall his subscribing to boxing magazines, his exercise gadgets, and his roadwork regime before supper. But he was too young to box; he was 17 and you had to be 18, so he went under my brother Joe's name as a welterweight at 147 pounds. He fought six amateur fights at the Cambria, a small, local fighting establishment at Kensington and Cambria Avenues and won them all, four by decision and two by knockout. I remember how excited my three brothers were when they returned home after a victory. They persuaded Pop to see Stan's next fight at the Arena in downtown

Philadelphia, against a lanky southpaw, with a Jewish sounding name, according to my brother Joe. Stan had the guy beat, according to Joe. In fact, he floored the guy in the fifth round for a count of nine. But he got off the floor and out of desperation he let go a roundhouse left-hander that caught Stan flush in the nose, breaking it badly, and letting loose a stream of blood. The referee called the fight and awarded Stan's opponent a TKO. That was the end of Stan's fighting career. Year's later he had plastic surgery done on his nose, but it didn't seem to improve his appearance much.

Soon after, Stan, with some encouragement from my father, joined the CCC, the Civilian Conservation Corps, part of President Franklin D. Roosevelt's New Deal to combat the unemployment of the Depression. The CCC was a paramilitary organization. The recruits were given dark green clothing, their food and shelter. They lived in barracks, followed a rigid daily schedule and were paid $50 a month. Stan signed up for a year. He was sent to the Pocono Mountain area, about 40 miles north of Philadelphia, where the CCC was carving highways out of the wilderness. Every month Stan would send home $40 of his pay for Pop to hold for him, and he sent home extra winter clothing he was assigned for us to wear. From his letters it was clear that he didn't like the CCC but that he had to tolerate it. At the end of the year, Stan came home and asked for his money that he sent home every month. My father was very much ashamed of himself, I remember, to have to admit that he did not have the money, that he spent it on household expenses, and, possibly, on a few binges. Stan was crushed. Soon after, he left home for the West Coast to work in the Kaiser Shipyards in Seattle. Then he moved to the desert area of New Mexico to work for the railroad, laying tracks. We lost contact with him for a number of years and sometimes wondered whether he was alive. We made a concerted effort to locate him when Pop was dying of cancer. We located Stan in New Mexico and informed him of Pop's condition. He returned home by car a few days after Pop died. He took good care of my mother for a few years after Pop's death. He brought his common-law wife east from New Mexico; fathered and brought up five children and died of an aneurysm about 10 years ago. I now play the role of surrogate father to four of the five children. One of the children, Ronnie, died a few years ago of cancer.

8

Every Sunday morning after the ten-thirty Mass during the warmer months, we were in a quandary: Where to play cards? Sometimes we played outside Mr. Furtek's home right in the middle of Mercer Street, just off Allegheny Avenue. This site invited trouble. We would have one eye on the cards and pot and one eye on Allegheny Avenue, watching for police cruisers. Inevitably, within an hour or so, a police car would turn into Mercer Street. Someone would holler, "Cheez it! The cops!" We would scatter in every direction: through the nearby alleyway that led to Almond Street; down the length of Mercer Street, back towards the police car to Allegheny Avenue. The policemen would get out, make a gesture at trying to catch somebody, pick up what money was still on the ground, pick up and tear the playing cards and take off. We would reassemble after about 10 minutes, bring out a new deck of cards and commence playing again. This would happen once, twice, sometimes three times every Sunday.

To avoid this nuisance, we could play cards in Furtek's driveway. The advantage was that we were hidden from the police cruisers cruising up and down Allegheny Avenue. The disadvantage was that if the police cruiser did find out we were playing there (After a while, the veteran cops figured if we weren't playing in the middle of Mercer Street, we must be playing in Furtek's driveway.) and came in after us, we were totally surprised and trapped. The driveway was large enough for the police car to roll in, with about three feet of room on each side of the car. When we saw the police cruiser roll in, we panicked. What to do? All we could do was rush the police car and hope the cops were more interested in picking up the money from the ground than arresting someone. And if they were interested in arresting someone, hope it wasn't you. Luckily, I was never taken to the police station, at least not for playing cards. But that possibility was always there when we played cards on Sunday morning after the ten-thirty Mass.

Googoo was the only one who had an alternate escape plan when the cops surprised us while playing cards in Furtek's driveway. He climbed on to the roof of the garages. I watched him in amazement as he jumped up, grabbed the hinge of the garage door with his right hand, lifted himself up to reach the top of the roof with his left hand, then lifted himself up on to the roof with both hands, and scrambled across to the Mercer Street side of the garages and freedom, even before the cops had time to get out of the car.

9

After dark, we also occasionally spent time doing mischief on the roof of Furtek's garages.. With a boost from one another, we would get on to the roof of the individual garages. Then we would go to the ladder that led to the roof of the three-story high truck garage. We just enjoyed the daring of it all. It was fun and scary to look down on Mercer Street, to call down to passersby, to throw small roof pebbles at your buddies who were too chicken to climb the roof to begin with. Mr. Furtek was infuriated with us. He would see us during the day and holler at us that we were damaging his roofs by running on them. He threatened to get the cops after us. But we never took him seriously.

There was a door that led from the truck garage on to the roof of the individual garages. It was always locked. One night the door opened and let out a beam of light. Out stepped Tommy, Mr. Furtek's recent son-in-law, husband of Bernadette, with a club in his hand. Cursing, swearing, with his eyes not yet accustomed to the dark, he ran after Beerzy, but couldn't catch him. He ran after Beebo and couldn't catch him. He ran after Reds and took one step too many. He ran off the roof. (What a horrific sensation that must have been!) We quickly got off the roof and ran by the prone Tommy, writhing in pain. Soon, an ambulance arrived. Tommy, we learned later, had a compound fracture of his left leg. He was in the Northeastern Hospital for about a month, wore a cast for several months and was disabled with a severe limp for the rest of his life. As cold and as insensitive as we were at that age, we were truly sorry for what we did to Tommy. Needless to say, it was the last time we played on Mr. Furtek's garages.

I thought maybe Bernadette and her husband Tommy, or their heirs, would have taken over the Furtek estate in reparation for Tommy's accident, but apparently they did not. It was all left to Joe and, later, to his wife.

10

In front of the Murawskis' home was the lone fire hydrant of the block. I don't recall that fire hydrant ever being used to provide us with fire protection, but it certainly provided us with relief from the heat on many hot summer days.. One of the older guys with an unofficial wrench would turn on the hydrant. First rusty water would come out followed by clear water and the word would spread: "The fire plug's on! The fire plug's on!" and all us kids in the block, screaming, laughing would kick off our sneakers and shirts and get under the water that was strong enough to knock some of us off our feet. Soon one of the older guys, usually Googoo, would embrace the hydrant and press his body against it, causing the water to form a shower that spanned the whole width of the street and we young kids would just frolic under it. It seemed just as we had enough fun and were sufficiently refreshed, as if by design, a water department truck would appear. All the big kids would run off in the opposite direction, and the water would be turned off, until another hot day and that mysterious, unofficial wrench appeared.

But we had other watery outlets on hot summer days. We had the bathos or bados (short for bathhouse), as we called the public swimming pool at Cohocksink Playground at Gaul and Ann Streets. Mondays, Wednesdays, and Fridays were Boys Days, and Tuesdays, Thursdays and Saturdays were Girls Days. Starting at 9:00 A.M., and every other hour afterward till 5:00 P.M., we could enjoy an hour's swim. To get in at 9:00 A.M., you had to get there early and stand in a long line. Once you got in, you undressed, got into your swimming trunks, ran through a shower and jumped into the pool. The pool was always packed. You could never dive into the pool and you could rarely jump into the pool without jumping on somebody. There was no room for swimming, above or below the water. All you could do was stay in the water, splash one another, and duck one another until the hour was up.

I still remember a deaf mute boy who seemed to be there whenever we were. He was older and bigger than we were who seemed to delight in tossing us smaller boys through the air. And the fact that he couldn't speak, just grunt and groan, made him more menacing. We were glad when he wasn't there. And we were glad if our clothes were still there when we finished swimming. You never took any valuables with you, not that we had any. To prevent you from swimming twice in one day, the lifeguards would feel your swimming trunks as you were about to enter. If they were wet, you were pulled out of line.

The Meadows was another water outlet for us who lived in a city with concrete and asphalt all around us. About an hour's walk north along the river towards Bridesburg, through Wheatsheaf (How this area got the name Wheatsheaf, I don't know. There certainly were no sheaves of wheat in our time.) through factory yards, over cinder piles, over railroads, under railroad cars we finally arrived at an oasis with a lagoon-like lake in its midst. The Meadows was a body of water about 150 yards in circumference. Near the shore it was thick with foliage that grew in water. There were palms and punks that we took home with us because it was believed that lit punks kept mosquitoes away, and other wild growing flora. And ringing the Meadows were factories, no doubt polluting it, as became obvious through the years.

Before my generation the Meadows was a haven. It was a mecca for fishermen fishing for goldfish. There were always dozens of fishermen with their homemade fishing poles and there were dozens more swimming in clean water on sandy bottoms. The clean water seeped in from the nearby Delaware River to the east and seeped out into rivulets. But then pollution from the factories ringing the Meadows also began to pour in. The fishermen were dismayed to find more and more goldfish floating dead on the surface of the water. The water was no longer clean. You couldn't see your hand six inches under water. The once sandy bottom was now a glue-like muddy substance; you dared not open your mouth in the water or swim under water. But in desperation we would still go swimming there only to find ring worms in our groin and armpits the next day.

The Boulevard Pools was another watery outlet for us. You had to take the 73 trolley and the 66 bus to get to Cottman and Frankford Avenues in the Torresdale section of Philadelphia, about 10 miles north in what is now called the Greater Northeast. But you had to pay 50 cents admission. The transportation and admission was too much for us. Word got around that there were holes under the chain-link fence surrounding the picnic area of the pool. So one early summer morning with our swimming trunks under our arms, with 20 cents in our pocket for transportation to and from, we set out to sneak into the Boulevard Pools. Sure enough, about halfway around the fence, we saw a hole just big enough for a small body, with some difficulty, to sneak through. We got into our trunks, bundled our clothes in a heap near the hole, put some leaves on them and easily blended in with the picnickers. We had a delightful time jumping and diving off the diving boards of various heights. We had plenty of space to swim, to play tag, to duck one another, to place a companion on your shoulders and to try to knock over other kids similarly conveyed, and we had all the time in the world. There was no lifeguard with a whistle telling us to get out after 45 minutes. This was no bathos.

Exhausted and hungry, we decided we had enough. We returned to our place of entry only to find our clothes gone, along with whatever money we had to get back home. We had no choice but to crawl under the fence again, laugh at how we were outwitted and pretend we were cross-country runners as we walked, jogged and ran our way home in our swimming trunks and bare feet.

After this episode at the Boulevard Pools, the next time, we stayed on the bus to Pennypack Circle, about a mile beyond the Boulevard Pools stop. We then would walk about a quarter of a mile to Pennypack Creek. It was a nice place to swim and it was free. It really was a creek, all in its pristine state. We walked over grass and stones from the dressing rooms to get to the swimming areas. We walked over stones in the creek to get to a depth where we could swim, where we could dive from a boulder in the middle of the creek. And after swimming, we could get dressed and explore the rest of the creek by just walking alongside it through the woods. The only man-made object in the whole setup were the dressing rooms: one for boys and one for girls. On this particular day, Beerzy pried open a knot in the boards between the two dressing areas. We began taking turns peeking through it. It was my turn. The girls must have heard us and stopped undressing. Instead, just as I took my eye away from the knothole, the end of a girl's comb came through the hole. That was a close call, and it would have been embarrassing. How would I explain how I got a punctured eye?

11

The Delaware River was our other outlet to make the dog days of summer tolerable. It was no Mark Twain's Mississippi River with its width and wilderness and its steamboats. But it was the next best thing to the Mississippi River for us. We had freighters from other countries bringing their goods to factories in South Philadelphia. We had tugboats and rowboats with fishermen dotting the river and we had fishermen with homemade fishing poles fishing from the edge of the pier. We had swimmers swimming off the edge of the pier and we had a sandbar near the Jersey side of the river with sand cleaner and finer than the sand at Wildwood or Atlantic City, two summer beach resorts in New Jersey. It was a comparatively short 10-minute walk to the river from where we hung out at Mercer and Allegheny Avenue.

One summer morning with somehow 50 cents between us, enough to rent a row-boat that fishermen rented for the day, Reds and I decided to rent a rowboat and row out to the sandbar and maybe make a day of it. With anticipation of enjoying the sandbar that we could barely see from the pier and leaving our sneakers as collateral, full of excitement we pushed out from the shore and began to row, somewhat in unison. Although Reds was my age and we were probably of equal weight and height, Reds was all muscle and I was still mostly baby fat. We rowed about a hundred yards from shore when we noticed a freighter about a half-mile to the left, moving south towards us.

"Reds, I think we better wait until the freighter passes."

"Naw, I don't think so. We can make it, Wimp."

"I don't think so, Reds."

This debate went on for several minutes until we decided to try it. We soon found out, as the freighter loomed larger and larger to our left, that we had made a mistake. The freighter blew a warning signal. We then began to panic. Our oars were no longer in sync; we were rowing in semi-circles, first to the left and then, to correct our direction, to the right. The freighter blew two quick warning signals. The faster, the harder we rowed, the less distance we were making it seemed. I thought for sure we were to be run over. Finally, a scant 30-40 feet away, the freighter came to a full stop and even seemed to go backwards a bit. We looked up in awe, at this dark metal wall, with a foreign inscription on its bow, towering over us. The bearded captain in a nautical cap and in a white short-sleeved shirt, leaning over the railing at the very front of the boat, with a foreign accent bellowed over a megaphone down at us. "Get along. Get along. Be careful next time. You can be killed."

Now more composed and in sync, we rowed out of the freighter's path. We could see the crew members smiling at us and waving at us. They even sounded a parting blast from its horn as the freighter resumed its journey to some South Philadelphia plant to unload its cargo and we continued on our way to the sandbar.

The sandbar was everything we were told about it. The sand was unbelievably clean and pure white that glistened and sparkled under the sun. We pulled the boat on to the sandbar. We walked around it, examining almost every inch, reveling in the fact that we were its sole inhabitants. We lay down and basked in the sun. We took off our clothes and swam, not fearing about being caught naked. Luckily, we noticed in time that the boat was slipping back in the water and the sandbar was getting smaller, which meant the tide was coming in rather rapidly and maybe, we thought, it was time to move on. Reluctantly, we pushed off and left our paradise.

But it was too early to turn in the rowboat. We wanted to get our full 50 cents worth, so we decided to float up the river and enjoy the sights which consisted mainly of factories. We hardly had to put an oar in the water as we floated northward with the tide to Bridesburg and then to Tacony and the five-cent (free on Christmas) toll Tacony-Palmyra Bridge. That's when we decided to turn around and head back home. It was already getting dark. But to our dismay, we found it a lot harder, if not impossible, to row against the current. For every three feet we gained with a stroke of the oars, we fell back two feet while preparing the oars for another stroke. Still, we tried rowing against the current for about an hour. We were tired, our hands were blistered, and soon the blisters broke and they began to bleed and all we had to show for it was about 200 yards towards home and we still had about two miles to go before we reached our destination: Port Richmond.

We decided on a different tactic. We rowed to the closest pier on the Philadelphia side of the river and pulled the boat along the pier. We found we made better time doing this rather than trying to row against the current. The sun had set; the wind was cold. We thought of abandoning the boat and walking home but we would forfeit our sneakers and the fellow who rented us the boat seemed like a nice guy and we would never be able to rent another boat in the future. So we pulled on from pier to pier, from dock to dock, from concrete embankment to concrete embankment until we finally arrived at Port Richmond.

We were relieved; the owner of the boat who stayed open longer for us was relieved. He said he began to worry about us. Reds and I walked home. I succeeded in hiding my bloody hands from my mother. Luckily, my father was working second shift. My mother merely asked me where I was all day and was I hungry. She gave me something to eat, and I went to bed exhausted.

12

Today, the area bounded on the east by the Delaware River and on the west by Richmond Street and bounded on the north by Westmoreland Street and on the south by Allegheny Avenue, except for a small playground on the corner of Allegheny Avenue and Richmond Street, is no longer accessible to pedestrians. An I-95 exit takes up quite a bit of space and the rest of space is taken up by trucking companies, all cordoning off their trucks and their terminals. Nobody, today, can walk to our Port Richmond pier and our beloved Delaware River as we did in our day. That whole area was our playground. We played hide-and-seek and "you're it" (our name for tag) in a lumberyard. We jumped off the roof of Harry Gransback Sand & Gravel Co. We tight-roped over railroad tracks over a twenty-foot hole filled with putrid rainwater and chemicals.

We enjoyed playing "hide-and-seek" and playing "you're it" in this lumberyard. We enjoyed jumping from pile to pile of lumber; we enjoyed taking a plank of lumber and forming a bridge from one pile of lumber to another; we enjoyed taking a plank to help climb up a higher pile of lumber. In the meantime, sometimes we would accidentally knock down a pile of lumber but we didn't care, sometimes we would get splinters in our hands and buttocks, and we did care. But we enjoyed even more avoiding the watchman of this lumberyard, who patrolled it on horseback. The horse was not very fast and he couldn't get into the nooks and crannies of these lumber piles nor could he climb them. The watchman was frustrated; he would threaten us, curse us and swear he would get us someday.

Off we went, one summer day to play in the lumberyard, a short ten minute walk from our homes, and to harass the watchman. We did our usual thing. Jumped from one pile of stacked lumber to another; formed bridges from one pile to another; hid from one another; tried to chase and touch one another; and then he whom you touched would join you in trying to touch others. The last one not touched was the winner. That was our game of "you're it," or tag. We were hoping the watchman would show up on horseback to add spice to our enjoyment. Instead, we heard the barking of a dog in the distance and soon found ourselves confronted by a snarling, growling, unleashed German shepherd, followed by the watchman on horseback. This was serious business; this was no joke. "How the hell do we get out of this lumberyard without being attacked by this dog?" we asked one another. We continued playing "hide-and-seek" but now it was with the German shepherd and we continued playing "you're it" but now "it" was the German shepherd. We dared not be touched by him. He still couldn't climb up these 20-30 foot piles of lumber, but he could keep us at bay and that he did until 5 o'clock when the watchman, frustrated, went home for the day. We got out of there as quickly as possible and that was the end of our playing "hide and seek" and "you're it" in the lumberyard.

Most of our death-defying games had to deal with heights and I was always and still am afraid of heights. But that was no excuse with the other kids. If you didn't do what they did, you were chicken. In this makeshift playground of ours, near the river, was another favorite place of ours: Harry Gransback Sand & Gravel Co., (I still remember the name. Probably because my experiences there were so traumatic.) on the right or southside of Allegheny, near the river, about 100 feet from the beginning of the pier. Often, during the day, all the trucks were out delivering and we had the place to ourselves. We were always climbing heights and jumping into piles of sand. Most of these heights were not so high except for one. A fresh pile of sand was dumped at the base of the office building itself, near the entrance. The office building was empty. Beebo suggested we jump from the pointed roof of the office building into the new pile of sand. There were cinderblocks piled up against the other end of the building. We climbed the cinderblocks, lifted ourselves up to the lowest point of the roof; climbed to the peak of the roof and then, straddling the peak, walked (Not I. I sat and inched my way forward.) the full length of the roof to the end where the new pile of sand was.

Maybe others were terrified but they didn't show it. Beebo was the first to go off. No problem. With a gesture of bravado, he jumped upwards and outwards from the roof with arms extended, hollering a war cry. (It's a wonder he didn't do a flip). Then Beerzy; then little Socko; then daredevil Baldy jumped; then, finally, it was my turn. I was sitting on the peak of the roof in a straddling position, inching closer to the edge. It wasn't too bad as long as I could see and touch the roof in front of me. But when I inched to the edge of the roof and still in a sitting position, leaned over to look down at the upturned, taunting faces of my "buddies" and looked at what seemed like a small pile of sand, I was filled with terror. I must have been 50 feet in the air but it seemed like 500 to me. I paused and said, "I'm not jumpin'. I'm comin' down." They taunted me further, calling me "chicken, a yellow belly," telling me to "hurry up and jump; the trucks will start comin' back." I finally stood up and stood on the edge of the roof, closed my eyes, said a quick Act of Contrition so I wouldn't go to hell if I died, and jumped. I landed clumsily on my feet. I fell forward with my upper body and my head ended up buried in sand. My buddies helped me out of the pile of sand, brushed me off, and congratulated me on my bravery.

I should have remembered that my head would go forward upon impact in this jump. Several years earlier Beebo and I, when we were six or seven, took some cardboard beer and liquor advertisements from his grandfather's trash pile outside his bar, Bosak's, on the corner of Almond and Allegheny, just one street west of Mercer Street. Beebo had the bright idea of seeing which one of us could push these advertisement displays higher up the 5-foot wide alley behind the bar building.

Sure enough, we found two cardboard beer advertisements that snugly fit between the two brick walls of the alley that extended up three stories. This should be fun, I thought, but again height began to play a part. We slipped off our sneakers (Our bare feet provided better traction than our worn sneakers.), pushed the advertisements with our hands above our heads as much as we could. Then we started our climb up the walls of the alley. With our legs and arms stretched to touch both walls, with feet and hands we pushed ourselves upward, upward, all the time pushing the advertisements above us higher with our hands and sometimes with our heads. Beebo, of course, was well ahead of me, nearing the third floor roof when I was approaching the second floor height, about 30 feet. I began to get nervous. I was about as high as I was going to go. I was about ready to start sliding down the sides of the alley, when Beebo suddenly in a shrill voice hollered, "Here come the Indians!" Startled, I lost my concentration, lost my grip on the walls, and fell to the ground like a rock. I landed on my feet but with impact I fell forward on my chin. I was dazed and when I saw blood all over my shirt, all over my hands, I began to cry. Beebo slid down and ran into his grandfather's bar. Luckily, my brother Joe was there. He ran out, picked me up and asked Adam Zagorski who was parking his father's butter and eggs delivery truck on Allegheny Avenue, next to Bosak's, to rush me to the Northeastern Hospital, about five minutes away. Joe got some blood on his clothes; even Adam got blood on his white uniform that he always wore when delivering butter and eggs for his father's business. I was taken to emergency, got stitched up and was fine. I still have a visible scar on my chin that prevents me from using a wet razor. And I never got a chance to thank Adam Zagorski. I was too young to know enough to thank him when I saw him carrying his golf clubs to his car one Saturday morning. Later, I never got a chance. He was killed in the invasion of Normandy.

There was another "death-defying" game we kids played in this area near the river that we regarded as our playground. We often would walk on railroad tracks to see who could stay on the longest and, of course, Beebo usually won. But if you fell off, it was nothing. You just stepped back on the tracks and tried again. But one section of these abandoned tracks had a craterlike hole under it. The hole was about 10 feet deep and about 20 feet long. At the bottom of the hole, there was about five feet of a stagnant, smelly substance. Of course, this presented a challenge, a dare. Who would dare walk those railroad tracks over that hole? We looked at the hole; we practiced over ground. We could easily walk 20 feet of railroad track over *terra firma* but not over that gaping black hole. No one accepted the challenge except, of course, Beebo. All of us watched breathlessly on the sidelines as Beebo started his walk over the hole. He had no stick to balance himself and he had no net if he fell. I think even Beebo was frightened with this challenge. Beebo must have his limits, I thought. He started out slowly, cautiously, not the way we almost ran on railroad tracks. He used his extended arms to steady himself. He took three steps; paused, and then stepped backwards a step. Over the middle of the hole, he lost his balance and almost fell off. He flailed his arms wildly trying to regain his balance. He did. Beebo walked a few more feet, then almost ran the last ten feet effortlessly, as if he were walking over solid ground.

Some of this area between Richmond Street and the river was also a source of income for us. That's where we would "go junkin'." Some parts of the area, especially closer to Westmoreland Street, were used as a dump by the nearby factories and when we needed some money we would "go junkin'" to the dump and look for metal we could sell at Sullivan's Junk Shop on Westmoreland and Edgemont Streets. (It is still there.) We would rummage through piles of discarded materials, looking for copper, brass, aluminum, even iron pieces. Sometimes, the material we were rummaging through was still smoldering, still hot. We looked for aluminum because it was fairly plentiful and paid the most: about 40 cents a pound. (Prices fluctuated every day, like the stock market.) Copper was also good, about 30 cents a pound, and, of course, it was heavier than aluminum. Brass was heavy, plentiful and paid about 20 cents a pound. Iron paid 5 cents a pound. It was hardly worth our effort to carry iron from the dump to Sullivan's. Sometimes, if we were lucky, we found pewter pieces that resembled aluminum but were heavier, slightly duller and worth a lot more than aluminum. When somebody found pewter, it was as if he had found gold. The news spread through the neighborhood. "Where? What dump? Let's go." We would rush to that particular pile, digging deeper, hoping to uncover more pewter.

13

Trains, and I don't mean toy Lionel trains, which were practically non-existent in our neighborhood during our times, played a significant part in our lives. I mean the slow moving, cargo-carrying, industrial trains that ran north and south along the Delaware River, delivering goods from the freighters to terminals up and down the river. I mean trains that ran east and west from these terminals to factories along the cobblestoned and train-tracked streets of Westmoreland, Tioga and other east-west arteries that ran through Port Richmond. I mean the high-speed passenger trains that ran from New York City to Philadelphia over multiple tracks located about two miles north of Port Richmond in the Erie-Torresdale area.

We found train-hopping exciting because it was dangerous, which was usually the case: we equated dangerous with exciting. We would run along a slow-moving industrial train moving along the river and grab hold of one of the ladders that lead to the top of the cars. We never knew when the train would start moving or for what distance, so we waited until it did start moving and got going to a fairly good clip. Then we knew it was likely not to stop soon. We would lift ourselves up a couple of rungs, hang on with one hand and wave to one another with the other. We would then enjoy a ride for several hundred yards or more, until the train came to one of its frequent stops, or until we saw one of the ever-lurking railroad "dicks" (cops) in the distance. Then it was time to get off which was no easy matter if the train were jouncing along at its top speed of about 10 miles an hour. You had to be careful when boarding, especially when putting your foot on the bottom rung of the ladder, not to miss the rung and put your foot through it. Your foot then came dangerously close to the wheel of the train. Getting off was even trickier. We ran as fast as we could when our feet hit the ground. Sometimes we couldn't keep up with our own momentum and we would stumble and tumble to the ground.

We never bothered hopping rides, although we were tempted many times, on the industrial trains running east and west on Westmoreland, Tioga and other east-west streets running through Port Richmond because these trains were going through populated areas and intersections and went too slow and stopped too frequently for it to be exciting. We were also concerned about being recognized by neighbors and reported to our parents for "train-hopping."

Our train-hopping exploits received a real jolt one day, a jolt severe enough to put a stop to our train-hopping. Ralphie Mocniak, about 10 years old, a few years younger than we, had both his legs mangled just under the knees while train-hopping. Apparently, while disembarking from a moving train, he tumbled under the wheels of the train. Luckily, a train "dick" nearby witnessed the accident. He quickly applied tourniquets to both legs, rushed him to Northeastern Hospital where they amputated both his legs just under the knees. I have seen Ralphie a number of times since the accident. At first, he was traumatized, as were we, but now he has adjusted nicely. He has reared a nice family, has owned and operated a successful neighborhood restaurant, with the help of two of his sons, for many years. The only after effect of the accident, because of the prostheses, is that he limps slightly. His accident marked the end of our train-hopping days but not our fascination with trains.

One summer day word got around that pewter was found in the dumps near the Erie-Torresdale train tracks, the same train tracks that my older brother Joe, to save a dime for carfare, traversed to get to nearby Northeast Catholic High School. Beerzy, Sajo, Socko and I walked the two-miles to the dump. We searched and searched and found nothing. The only thing we found were several unopened boxes of cookies, discarded by nearby TastyKake Baking Co. We opened a few boxes, carefully examined the contents, found that they looked and smelled good. We ate them, while sitting along about 20 sets of tracks, watching high-speed passenger trains coming from New York City to North Philadelphia Station and to 30th Street

Station in Center Philadelphia. We waved happily to the passengers and some responded.

Sajo noticed about a 100 yards in the distance that the Frankford El above the tracks was supported by two massive concrete pillars or abutments, the foundations of which formed platforms about 6 feet above the ground and about 6 feet by 6 feet in area. Sajo suggested, "Let's climb up to the platform and wave to the people in the trains passing by." "Why not?" said Little Socko. It seemed we climbed anything that was climbable. We boosted one another up to the platform and finally pulled Beerzy up. We just had about enough room to move around. When a train on a distant track went by, we waved to it and passengers, who now could see us better on the platform, waved back. When another train, closer to where we were, went by, we noticed a surge of wind generated by the velocity of the train, which startled us. And when a train ran immediately by the pillar we were standing on, we were all slightly unnerved. The next time a nearby train came by we all embraced one another and we all embraced the pillar. The rush of wind was so severe. Sajo, the thinnest and lightest of us all, said, "Let 's get the f... off this thing before we're blown off." Just then we caught sight of two trains in the distance, alongside each other, equidistant to us that appeared to be running on the two tracks alongside both sides of the pillar-platform we were standing on. It was too late to get down. We had to brave the wind that was about to hit us. Sajo and Socko embraced the pillar, clutching the rough-hewn sides of the pillar. Beerzy looked back one final time and said, "Holy shit, here they come!" He and I embraced Sajo and Socko with one arm and held on to the sides of the rough-hewn pillar with the other, protecting them and us from the impending wind the best we could. The two trains arrived simultaneously. The wind from the trains buffeted us from side to side. It was as if we were caught in a powerful wind tunnel. And, in this case, it is no cliché to say: WE HELD ON FOR DEAR LIFE! I felt sure we were going to die. But we survived. Surprisingly, it was the deafening noise rather than the wind that was more frightening, more overwhelming. The trains must have been extra long because the wind and noise lasted about 10 seconds, which, to us, seemed like 10 minutes. That was our one and only experience with high-speed passenger trains.

But that was not my last view of those 20 or so pairs of tracks and the trains that whizzed by on them. Two years later I would revisit this scene from a different perspective: from the overhead Frankford elevated train. In early September of 1943, when I was 14 years old, I nervously awaited the next morning: my first day at Northeast Catholic High School, just a short walk from the Erie-Torresdale El Station. That evening after supper, as Walt was washing up for a date with his future wife Ann, the radio announcer issued a call for all men with welding and burning torch experience to report to the train tracks near Erie and Torresdale Avenues. A terrific train wreck occurred, taking the lives of scores of people. It seemed that a high-speed passenger train from New York City left the tracks. Volunteers with burning torch skills were needed to extricate the victims and the survivors. Walt, who was a welder/burner at the Philadelphia Navy Yard in South Philadelphia, quickly changed his plans for the evening. He hopped in the family car out front and spent that evening and most of the early morning burning through train wreckage in an effort to reach victims and survivors alike. The next morning Walt slept in and did not go to work at the Philadelphia Navy Yard. I got up early for my first day of high school. I boarded the 60 trolley car at Thompson and Allegheny, took it to Kensington and Allegheny, boarded the northbound Frankford El to the Erie and Torresdale Station, just two stops north. As we approached the Erie and Torresdale Station, the El came to a standstill to allow us to view the wreckage, the carnage. Volunteer rescuers were still milling about. The still smoldering engine was lying on its side. Trains were heaped upon trains, forming several triangular shapes about 50 feet in the air and about 50 feet from that pillar we stood on two years ago.

14

To make money, sometimes we sold paper to Sullivan's. Some would pick up the paper from the trash left out front by neighbors. About once a month I would collect the papers in the house, tie them up in a bundle and take them to Sullivan's and get my 10 or 20 cents, usually enough to buy some candy or get me into the Saturday movies at the Richmond theater. Sometimes, to make the paper heavier (I learned this trick from my older brothers.), I would wet some of the paper and place the wet paper in the middle of the bundle. Other times, I went so far as to place a brick in the middle of the bundle. But it wasn't long before the Sullivan boys got wise to our shenanigans and began opening our bundles before they weighed them. It was mighty embarrassing, even for us young kids, to have a brick found in the middle of your bundle of paper.

Another way of making some money was to shine shoes on Friday and Saturday nights. We would build our shoeshine box out of scraps of wood, nail a leather strap on it to place the strap across our shoulder as we walked from bar to bar in the neighborhood. There was some original expense to get started. We had to buy the necessary supplies: brown and black cans of cleansing polish, brown and black cans of wax polish, brown and black dauber brushes, brown and black shining brushes, and brown and black shining rags. The saliva was free. We walked into a crowded bar, went along the bar, looking for a dirty pair of shoes. When we found a pair, we asked, "Want a shine, mister? You really need a shine." The man would look down at his shoes and say, "Go ahead, kid," and continue talking and drinking his beer. We rolled up his pant cuffs so as not to get any polish on his trousers and shined away. The price of a shoeshine was 15 cents. Most gave you a quarter and drunks often gave you more. If we had a good night, we could make as much as ten dollars on a Friday or Saturday night.

There was an even easier way to get rich: shoplifting. Older fellows from the gang would show off their loot: shiny, new, expensive accessories for bicycles and automobiles from Pep Boys; combs, cards, inexpensive jewelry from Woolworth's and Kresge's five-and-dimes on Kensington Avenue; bigger and more expensive stuff from Sears & Roebuck on the Boulevard. Our eyes would bulge out of our sockets looking at this almost daily treasure trove, especially from Pep Boys. It's a wonder Pep Boys, from this first and original store, eventually expanded nationally, so much was stolen from them by guys in our neighborhood alone. But like all good things, shoplifting quickly came to an end when the store owners began to crack down and post plainclothes store security guards in their stores. All it took was the word to get around that so and so was caught shoplifting and was arrested for it to end.

Some of the older fellows tried to make money legitimately, by huckstering. They would rent a horse and wagon for the day for twenty dollars. Early in the morning, they would go to the market on Delaware Avenue near the river, buy up, at wholesale prices, all kinds of produce and sell it throughout the neighborhood. Shooey, Beerzy's older brother, and Huntzy recruited me to help them huckster. While they worked the streets, I would work the alleys between rows of houses. I would holler out, "Huckster! Huckster! Jerzee tomatee! Red ripe watermellow! Red ripe strawwwberreee!" and when a woman came out and gave me her order, I would run out to the wagon to get whatever she ordered.

It was a long, disappointing day. We sold only about half of our load and dumped the remaining half at a lot near Aramingo and Ontario. Shooey and Huntzy decided to have some fun before they turned in the horse and wagon at the end of the day. Back then Aramingo beyond Ontario Street was unpaved. It was a dirt road, with large, deep ruts in it. It was virtually impassable to cars. We started at Ontario Street. Shooey gave the horse a sharp snap of the reins over the back. The horse took off in a hurry. Imitating the cowboys of the movies, I suppose, Shooey, hollering at the horse, sat on the front seat of the wagon, Huntsy riding shotgun alongside of him, and I bouncing around in the back of the wagon, holding on for dear life as the wagon and I literally were bouncing in the air. Shooey continued to flog the horse unmercifully and to get the horse to go even faster, he slapped the horse viciously underneath his belly across his testicles. The horse, then, really took off in a full gallop. You would never think he was pulling a wagon behind him. I'm certain it was the fastest that horse ever ran in its lifetime. The faster the horse ran, the more Shooey and Huntzy hooped and hollered and the more I bounced around in the back of the wagon. It's a wonder the wagon stayed intact. It was exciting while it lasted but it was probably inhumane as far as the horse was concerned. They paid me fifty cents instead of the dollar they promised. But the ride down Aramingo Avenue made it all seem worthwhile to me.

15

I met Shooey many years later a few days after I was ordained a priest. Because the chaplain at the Sacred Heart Home for Incurable Cancer Patients, was a gruff, old, lovable priest, Fr. Herman Buckley, who lived at nearby Northeast Catholic High School, it was customary for newly-ordained Oblate priests in the Phildelphia area to say one of their first Masses at the Home, bring Holy Communion to the patients and give them your First Blessing. I hardly recognized Shooey as I gave him Holy Communion; he was so emaciated. I had difficulty distributing Communion to many of the patients. Their faces were badly disfigured and had multiple holes in their faces. The Nun holding the paten had to direct me where to place the Host. I didn't know which hole was their mouth. The stench, the odor of death, of rotting flesh was everywhere. After being served a sumptuous breakfast of fried eggs, bacon, sausage, toast, coffee and juice, which I didn't touch for fear I would regurgitate, I went back and visited with Shooey and visited him a number of times after that. His case was so sad. He had a form of colon cancer that was terminal. When I would visit him, he was always covered by a sheet with only his head exposed. On several occasions he told me, moving his hands underneath the sheet, that, to his dismay, he discovered a "new hole" in his body. He wanted to live so desperately: "Wimp! Wimp! I just want to live to see my two boys grow up. Can you help me?" I prayed for a miracle, but it wasn't to be. In fact, I applied a relic of Fr. Louis Brisson, founder of the Oblates of St. Francis de Sales, whose cause for sainthood was, and still is, in process. Shooey died two months later. He was 38 years old. Personally, I think the order of nuns, founded by Rose Hawthorne, daughter of Nathaniel Hawthorne, famous 19th century American author, whose lifework is to staff these hospitals for incurable cancer patients, must all be saints.

16

We discovered another way of making money. At this time, there were very few telephones in private homes. In fact, it was an event when Sitko's Pharmacy on Allegheny Avenue, next to Majeski's, had three public telephones installed near the entrance of the pharmacy. We would sit outside the pharmacy and wait for a telephone to ring. We would take turns running into the pharmacy to answer the phone and ask for whom it was and where he or she lived. We would then run to that house, tell the occupant that he or she (mostly she) had a telephone call. Invariably, we would be tipped, a nickel, a dime, even sometimes a quarter. But this quickly got out of hand. Often, all three telephones were occupied this way and those who wanted to make an outgoing call had to wait. Mr. Sitko would not allow us to answer the phone when it rang and soon the callers and callees got the message, which was, not to make any incoming calls on these phones.

It wasn't too long before my older brothers talked my father into getting a phone so they could talk to their friends, particularly their girl friends. The party line was cheaper. Obviously, we got a party line, which created some problems. We couldn't use the phone if somebody on our party line was using it and when we got on the phone we always wondered who was listening in on our conversation. We knew they were listening in because we listened in on their conversations. It was a relief to get our own line, eventually.

When my wife and I went to Poland in November of 1999 to visit my cousins and see where my father was born and reared, I thought it was interesting that the day we visited my cousin's home where my father was born about a hundred years earlier was the first day his telephone was installed. It took more than 10 years after Communist rule to install telephone lines in the homes of this small hamlet of Karwowa near the city of Jedwabne in a rural area in northeast Poland, and it was about 60 years after we had our telephone installed in Philadelphia. We were there at my cousin Stan's home to witness (to hear?) an historic event: his first phone call from his sister, whose home we left just a few hours previously and who wanted to verify that we arrived safely.

17

It was about this time that I embarked on my short-lived accordion career. A traveling salesman from the Wurlitzer Company talked my father into signing me up for accordion lessons. The salesman left a spanking new accordion for me to practice on every day for an hour. Every Saturday morning at nine I was to be at their studios in downtown Philadelphia for lessons. Since Walt was next youngest, he was designated to accompany me to the lessons. As soon as we left the house, he would cuff me on the back of the head for being responsible for his having to get up so early on a Saturday morning. He didn't seem to realize that I wasn't too happy about getting up that early either.

I did well the first five or six Saturdays. I was getting a gold star pasted on my lessons book every Saturday until I moved on to Book Two of the lessons. Book Two did not have the little number above the notes. The numbers told you what fingers to use. I was cheating all this time, I guess, and didn't know it. I wasn't supposed to look at the numbers only the notes, but I was never told that. Without the numbers, I was lost. I was no longer getting gold stars, not even silver stars, not even a blue star. My father still insisted on my continuing the lessons and still practicing for an hour every afternoon, and Walt was still cuffing me around the head every Saturday morning on our way to downtown Philadelphia. I suppose my father had visions of my becoming an accordionist at Polish weddings where I the accordionist, along with the other two or three musicians, would introduce every new arrival at the reception-hall with a distinctive introductory tune, for which the new arrivals would handsomely tip the musicians. But I was not meant to be a musician. I much rather play with the other kids outside than practice the accordion. Eventually, my father gave up on me and returned the accordion to Wurlitzer.

I was surprised many years later, when as a priest, I was assigned to teach at Bishop Duffy High School in Niagara Falls, New York, to find that Wurlitzer's central headquarters and main manufacturing plant was located nearby in North Tonawanda. Wurlitzer was also one of the leading manufacturers of juke boxes in the country at the time.

18

The radio played a big part in our lives during this time. Our first radio was a Philco, a table model that was set in the middle of our long narrow living/dining room. I listened to many a baseball game, lying on my stomach on the floor. I often kept box score which meant I drew nine lines vertically for the innings and nine lines horizontally for the players. When a player hit a single, I placed a diagonal line in the upper right hand of the square; a double, two diagonal lines, upper right and left corners; a triple, another diagonal in the bottom right and a homer, a diagonal in all four corners. If the player flied out to right field, I placed an 0-7 in the square. If he grounded out from shortstop to first base, I wrote in 6-3. The defenders were all given a number: pitcher, 1; catcher, 2; first baseman, 3; second baseman, 4; third baseman 5; shortstop, 6; rightfielder, 7; centerfielder, 8, and leftfielder, 9. If the batter struck out, I placed a K in the square; if he walked, I placed a W.

Ed Chrzanowski

If I had the patience to keep the box score for an entire game, I would come to the corner or the park and wave it proudly to my envious friends. It was an achievement to have a box score of an entire game, particularly if the home team won. I listened to "Jack Armstrong, the All-American Boy" every day at 5 o'clock. I sometimes listened to the "Amos 'n Andy Show," "Fibber McGee and Molly Show," and "The Hit Parade Show" on Saturday nights. You always guessed which song would be number one for that week I listened, along with my brothers and sometimes my father, to Joe Louis's fights, especially against Max Schmeling, the German. I remember President Roosevelt's "Day of Infamy" speech when he announced the bombing of Pearl Harbor by the Japanese. I had to translate it for my mother and father that Sunday morning as I often translated his frequent fireside chats delivered over the radio. *"Co un mowi? Co un mowi?* What's he saying? What's he saying?" they would repeatedly ask and I would do my best to answer them, translating as he spoke. Roosevelt was a hero, a god, in my parents' eyes.

On Sunday afternoon I often wanted to listen to the scary "The Shadow" show, even though I didn't quite understand it most of the time. But my mother insisted on listening at the same time to "Fr. Justin's Rosary Hour" from Athol Springs, New York, and she usually won out. In fact, my mother often made me sit there and listen with her as Fr. Justin delivered a sermon in Polish, of course, and then recited the rosary, which she and I also recited with him. That was so boooooring. Years later, as a priest at Bishop Duffy High School in Niagara Falls, New York, I was surprised again to find that boring program from Athol Springs I was forced to listen to as a child originated from the other side of Buffalo, only about 25 miles away.

Our next radio was a floor model, an Atwater Kent, and our third model was another Philco but this time a fancy push-button model. I found it fascinating that we could change a station by just pushing a button. I didn't have to worry anymore about turning the knob to the right or left too much and breaking it, as my mother cautioned me every time I turned the knob.

19

It was about this time, in the fourth or fifth grade, that I recognized I was not very popular with the girls. I wondered why. I noticed I never smiled much in the presence of girls and I knew why. My front teeth were bad. I asked my mother if I could go to the dentist—a surprising request for a 10 or 11-year old. A young, new dentist, Dr. Roman, just opened a practice at the corner of Edgemont and Allegheny Avenue just across the street from the abandoned bank. His beautiful home was the lone property on the entire city block that was not owned by the parish. We went to him for another reason. My father knew his father from the Old Country and bought our shoes from him at his store on the corner of Richmond and Clementine Streets. After examining my teeth, Dr. Roman said the bill would be 28 dollars—a staggering amount at the time, equivalent to Pop's weekly pay. Mom agreed to pay him a dollar every visit. Every time I went to the doctor, a nice, handsome man with a beautiful, buxom, brunette wife who served as his assistant and receptionist, I would bring a dollar and he would drill a tooth for a few minutes and put in a temporary filling that would fall out within a few days. This went on for several months without his filling a single tooth permanently and I still wasn't getting anywhere with the girls. In fact, things got worse. My drilled cavities were bigger and the temporary fillings just called more attention to my bad teeth. I complained to my mother and asked if she could pay off the remainder of the bill. She gave me the balance. My next visit he filled my four front teeth permanently. I couldn't believe the transformation. It was as if I had a new set of teeth. I was a new person. The first person I smiled at was the dentist's wife and she smiled back. I never stopped smiling at the girls and all of a sudden I became very popular with them.

Every winter I would get a terrible sore throat and my breath stunk. The doctor diagnosed bad tonsils and recommended a tonsillectomy. But the procedure meant at least an overnight stay in the hospital, which my father couldn't afford. He delayed the operation at least a year until he heard of this doctor (?) in the Germantown area of Philadelphia who performed the procedure in his office for 25 dollars. His office was in a big, beautiful Victorian mansion. The foyer-entrance, which served as his waiting room, was high ceilinged with hardwood floors and dark wood paneling along the walls. The chairs along the walls were high-backed wooden chairs with plush crimson cushions. The next room, originally a dining room, served as the operating room.

I was scared. All I remember is the male nurse or doctor's assistant (He seemed too young to be a doctor.), who performed the operation, showed me the instrument he was going to use to snip off the tonsils. It looked like a pair of pliers with a metal noose at the end. He said the Indians used a similar device to catch fish. When the fish entered the noose, the Indians would squeeze the pliers and tighten the metal noose around the fish. That little anecdote did the trick. I was so distracted by this cute story and the utensil he was about to use, after a quick local anesthetic, he snipped my tonsils before I knew it.

I then remained in the waiting room for several hours sicker to my stomach than I had ever been before. I thought for sure I would vomit but I didn't. Finally, I went home, unable to talk, unable to swallow for several days—except for ice cream, which I was given all I wanted. I was the envy of all the guys as I met them at the corner licking on an ever-present ice cream cone.

20

There was another area of land that our imaginations turned into a playground, "the jungle," as we called it. The area, about a mile north of Allegheny Avenue, was undeveloped, except for an occasional factory or truck terminal. Most of the area was overgrown with thick bushes and trees and occasional boulders left over from the time the area was used as a dump. Today, it is fully developed with residential, commercial, and industrial properties. We enjoyed going there and pretending we were explorers pushing our way through this jungle. We pushed our way deep into this jungle, maybe a quarter of a mile, with stickers sticking to our clothing, vines cutting our skin, with poison ivy and poison oak all around us. After a while, we turned back to "civilization," lest we become lost.

This exploration of the jungle was a relatively harmless pastime until the advent of the BB gun craze. Then we stalked one another with BB guns. I was one of the last to get a BB gun. I begged my mother and father for one. They said they were too dangerous and too expensive. Lo and behold! My three skinflint older brothers pitched in together and bought me a brand new, shiny Daisy BB gun. It was not the best, but I was very happy with it. The best and most expensive was the Daisy Air Rifle. You could increase its velocity and accuracy by pulling back several times a sliding part on the underpart of the barrel of the gun. But with mine, I prepared to shoot by placing the handle of the gun under my leg and pulling up on a lever.

We were bored shooting at tin cans and bottles and occasional Furtek garage windows. We were going to shoot at humans, at one another. About a dozen of us marched to the "jungle," dressed in our heaviest jackets even though it was a warm day. We split up into sides. Six of us entered the jungle. After about 10 minutes, the other six hunted us down. We all realized the possibility of losing an eye, and it was our one, real fear, but the game was too exciting to not play because of this fear. And, anyway, there was one rule: You were not to shoot at anybody's face. So we played and stalked one another. It's as close as I have ever come to hunting or being hunted. We moved slowly, stealthily. I shot several adversaries several times and heard them cry out in pain. I recall being shot a number of times in my chest, in my arms, and remember the sharp pain I felt even though I was heavily clothed. I remember noticing the difference of pain inflicted by an Air Rifle and an ordinary Daisy BB gun. I tried not to expose just my head for fear of being shot in the face or the eye. But at one point in the hunt, I was hiding behind a huge, concrete slab with support irons sticking out of it, with only my face and shoulders exposed. I was shot in the face. I let out a scream. It was an Air Rifle. Another BB hit a support iron in front of my eyes. Somebody was not playing the game according to the rules, I thought. I quickly stood up and hollered, "I surrender." This was the only time we played this game in "the jungle." We realized, afterwards, how foolish and dangerous it was.

Ed Chrzanowski

I then turned my attention to shooting animals. We had a female cat that must have been in heat because it seemed all the male alley cats in our block were perched on our back fence, serenading her. As inhumane as it might seem, and it did bother me at the time, every day for several days I would rush home from school and from our upper back bedroom window, I shot at these cats. I must confess I took some delight when I saw a cat start, look around in bewilderment as to where the pellet was coming from. I didn't believe I was seriously hurting them. After a cat was hit once or twice, he left never to bother our cat and our serenity again.

21

We had other places to play besides the river and "the jungle," especially after dark. We found the front lawn of the parish rectory on Allegheny Avenue with its massive and neat rows of hedges an ideal place to play "hide and seek" and "you're it." We quietly opened the front iron gate leading to the rectory. We quietly made our rules and appointed who was to hide and who was to seek, who was "it" and who wasn't "it" and commenced to play. We played for hours, sneaking and running through hedges, hiding behind trees. No one bothered us. Occasionally, we would see a priest or parishioner entering or leaving the rectory, but that was all. It seemed that nobody even noticed that we were there, but we did notice that the holes we made in the hedges by constantly running through them were getting bigger and wider. But somebody must have noticed. The next night, Beerzy, running through a hedge, let out a scream. We rushed to him and saw him on the ground writhing with pain. His pants were torn and his upper legs bled profusely. He ran into barbed wire. We found all the hedges had been strung with barbed wire. I really and truly never forgave Msgr. Monkiewicz, the pastor, for doing that. He could have at least warned us, I thought.

During any summer morning all it would take to start a game of marbles would be for someone to suggest, "Let's shoot some marbles." We'd run to our homes to get our marbles. Those who didn't have marbles would harangue their mothers for a dime and go to Yeakel's Variety Store, on the corner of Miller Street and Allegheny Avenue, across from the German church, Our Lady Help of Christians. Mrs. Yeakell was ancient by our reckoning, too old and too nice to even try to steal from. She truly had a variety store. She had a little bit of everything. The store was capacious for a corner store. Mrs. Yeakel was tall, thin, gray-headed, bespectacled and wobbled when she walked and she spoke with a heavy German accent. She took care of the store alone all the time. She was grandmotherly nice to all us kids. When you opened the front door and the attached bell rang, she would rise from a seat behind the counter and pleasantly ask, "Vat can I get for you?" "A bag of marbles, please." She handed you a see-through, red-netted bag containing about 20 marbles, consisting of a couple of jumbos, a couple of pee-wees, and, hopefully, only a few agates, non-glossy inferior marbles, and the rest shooters, polished, slippery, shiny marbles. We carefully looked the marbles over to see if we liked the shine and design of the shooter marbles. If we did, we gave her the ten cents and off we ran to the park to shoot some marbles.

A five- or six- foot diameter circle was already etched in the dirt, probably first etched years ago. The grass in the circle and around the circle was long gone, trampled by marble shooters. We then shot our marbles from one end of the circle to the other to determine the order of shooters once the game started. Much like pool, the closest to the edge of the circle was the first to shoot, and we all hoped it wouldn't be Beebo.

We all put five of our shooter marbles in the center of the circle where there was a slight depression. Then the first shooter with his jumbo marble shot into the pile of 30, 35, 40 or more marbles, depending on how many players were in the game. If one of these marbles was knocked out of the circle, the shooter replaced his jumbo with a shooter marble and continued shooting until he failed to knock a marble out of the circle or when his shooter rolled out of the circle. Then the next shooter from the perimeter would shoot at the marbles closest to the perimeter, trying to work his way to the center where most of the marbles were.

Then came Beebo's turn. With his shooter held firmly in the crook of his index finger, and then released slightly just as his thumb flicked at the marble, jetting it forward. The secret was to have your shooter stop at the point it made contact with another marble; otherwise it would roll out of the circle after the marble it hit. Beebo had that knack of sticking his shooter. He started near the perimeter and worked his way to the center and the game was over. One after another marble, he knocked out of the circle, positioning himself for the next marble, much like in pocket billiards. We stood there helplessly, angrily watching as he was on his way to cleaning out the whole ring, without some of us even getting a single turn. With just a few marbles left, Beebo made the mistake of standing up to relax, to stretch his legs, to bask a little bit in his triumph, and, if the truth be told, to taunt us. It was at that point that Baldy said, "It's the shooter! Let's get the shooter!" And all of us, encircling the ring with our jumbos clenched in our right hands, started to throw at Beebo's shooter, like a scene out of William Goldman's *Lord of the Flies,* hoping to shatter it to smithereens, and we did. We blamed Beebo's success on the shooter, not on Beebo's uncanny ability. Beebo didn't care. He knew it wasn't the shooter and there were plenty more shooters where that one came from. It came to a point that we refused to shoot marbles if Beebo was going to shoot.

What Beebo did to us in shooting marbles, a few years later at the Polish American Social Club and at the Lithuanian Social Club he repeatedly did to us in shooting pool. The exact same thing. He would break the rack and often run the whole rack as we watched helplessly. This time we did not play for marbles; we didn't smash the cue ball; we just threw the money on the table, placed our cue stick back in the rack, and left in disgust. We often refused to shoot pool if Beebo was going to be in the game. I guess being as good as he was, might have been as tough, if not tougher, on Beebo as it was on us. But that was the price he paid for being so good at everything he did.

We also played Pom Pom Pullaway at the park in the evening. It replaced the game of Tiger. It amounted to the same rules as the "you're it" game, except it was not merely touching somebody, but tackling somebody. Whoever was "it," stood in the middle of a 50-foot section of the park, facing everybody else. We all ran at him at once and it was his objective to tackle one of us and that one would then assist the "it" person to tackle others as we ran back the other way. The game finally ended when the final person was tackled, usually gang tackled because he had everybody against him. Many a night I came home with a split lip, a sprained ankle, a scraped elbow, a bloody nose as a result of playing Pom Pom Pullaway, a very rough game that amounted to tackle football without the equipment of tackle football.

At the park, once every spring night, we played the devilish, mischievous, stupid game of tearing up newly-laid sod and throwing it at one another. What a terrible waste, what vandalism but we didn't know any better, I don't think. The city, every year, would lay sod, and every year we would uproot it before it had time to grow in and enjoyed throwing the clumps of sod at one another. It must have been terribly discouraging to the city park's people and to the people of Port Richmond to see their park vandalized that way. We should have been apprehended and punished but we never were.

Maybe the city authorities figured we needed some playground area to keep us out of such mischief, so they eventually started to clean up the area between Richmond Street and the Delaware River. Dumping was no longer allowed; the dumps already there were leveled and covered over. Other areas were fenced in and trespassers were not allowed. The lumberyard was gone. A few concession stands appeared at the foot of the pier. A few truck terminals appeared and a significant area adjacent to Richmond Street across from the Polish American Club on Allegheny Avenue was leveled, smoothed over and made into a baseball field. Finally, we had a long-awaited baseball field and with a backstop in the neighborhood.

Every day of summer, all day long, we played baseball. We chose sides if we had enough players or we would play "hit the bat" if we didn't. In "hit the bat," you took turns batting. If the ball you hit was caught on a fly, you were considered out and had to go out and play the field, starting in right field, and working your way through all the positions until it came time to bat again. You moved from position to position, first the outfield, then the infield, and finally the pitcher. If you hit a ball that was not caught in the air, you placed your bat in front of homeplate and the person who retrieved your ball rolled the ball in, trying to hit the bat. If he succeeded, you were out and had to play the field. If not, you had another turn at bat.

Sometimes we just practiced hitting and fielding. Shortstop was my favorite position. I imagined myself another Wayne Ambler (I just liked the name. He wasn't much of a shortstop.) of the Philadelphia A's. The other players did not think much of me as a shortstop either. In fact, they thought I was terrible and always wanted me to play elsewhere, but I insisted, until it dawned on me one day that they were right and I was wrong, that I was allowing more than half the balls through my legs and the ones I did stop, I threw over the first baseman's head. I saw the light. A shortstop I was not. Reluctantly, I went out to graze in right field

Those summer days were hot and I frequently became intensely thirsty. I couldn't wait to get home and have a beer. That's right. A beer. I must have been all of ten or eleven. My father always had five or six cold beers in the refrigerator. I came home, guzzled down a beer or two, and replaced them with beers from the shed. My mother and father were both working during this time. My father never seemed to miss a beer or two. But one week I did this every day for a full week and when my father checked on his supply in the shed Saturday morning, he did notice. "What happened to all the beer?" he screamed in Polish. I had to confess and was severely beaten with Pop's infamous strap. That was the end of my beer drinking days, at least for a few years.

22

In addition to fear of heights and dogs, another phobia I have is being hit in the face with a baseball while watching a baseball game. I know the origin of this phobia. It was the day Little Louie Pieroni, a slick-fielding second baseman, had his face smashed.

When the city installed the backstop at the baseball field at Richmond and Allegheny, they also scraped the infield, put in a pitcher's mound, leveled and planted grass in the outfield. The next year they added three rows of stands from homeplate to third base and to first base. Now we had a ball diamond worthy enough to play some organized baseball on, nice enough to attract and accommodate a crowd of several hundred people. The one thing the city neglected to do was to place a screen to protect the fans from foul balls.

I recall being part of the crowd on a Sunday afternoon, sitting in the third row of stands about 20 feet from homeplate on the third base side. Louie, a nice-looking kid about 18-years-old with an infectious smile. He played second base and he batted second. When he grounded out, he went to the stands on the third-base side to collect donations from the fans to help pay for the umpires, the equipment, and maintenance of the field. Lennie Wojtaszek, our slugging first basemen batting third, was at bat. Louie, with a big smile, flirting with the girls, stretched out his baseball cap to collect a donation. With a sickening thud, the vicious line drive foul ball hit Louie flush on the left side of the face just above the jaw. The ball fell inert next to Louie's prone, unconscious body, blood flowing from his mouth, his nostrils, his ears, and his left eye. This all happened five feet from me. I thought he was dead. We heard next day that he would survive but that his left jaw and cheek bone were shattered, most of his teeth were shattered and those that were not had to be extracted. His vision in his left eye was impaired.

Louie was in the hospital for about a month. He came out with his jaw still wired for several more months, able to drink and eat only through a straw, and left for life with a disfigured face, as if he had a severe stroke. And that was the end of Louie's promising baseball career. He never played again. He could never smile again. He wasn't handsome anymore. The next day after the accident, a day too late, the city put up chicken wire mesh from home plate to first and third base.

Ever since that accident, more than 50 years ago, I've been aware of what a baseball can do to you, how hard it is, how heavy it is, how it stings your hand even when caught with a baseball glove. To this day, I don't understand how fans at a baseball game reach out to catch a line-drive foul ball. Don't they realize the ball can break their fingers, their hand, their nose, their teeth? I still shudder when I see on television a line-drive foul ball hit into the stands and see all those unsuspecting fools trying to catch it. They should be cowering with fear, ducking their heads, protecting their faces with their arms.

Saying all that, I was amazed at my reaction a few years ago while attending a baseball game at Veterans

Stadium in Philadelphia between the Philadelphia Phillies and the Pittsburgh Pirates. My wife and I escorted three other couples from Lockport to visit the historical sites of Philadelphia. At the last minute we decided to take in a baseball game. We got seats in the upper-deck bleachers just inside the left-field foul line. As we took our seats, my wife, with whom I had shared my fear of getting hit with a batted ball at a game and now shared that fear with me, whispered to me, "What happens if a ball is hit to us?" To reassure her, and myself, I said, "Don't worry. They can't hit a ball this far."

In the fourth inning, Pete Incaviglia, an over-the-hill power hitter, now playing for the Phillies, unleashed a rocket-like line drive that I picked up with my eyes the instant the ball hit the bat and I followed the path of the ball all the way as it rose about 40 feet and on a line was heading right at me. I lost all fear; I never had any fear; I rose from my seat and excitedly awaited the ball. And like Ted Williams, who claimed he saw the seams on pitched balls, I swear I saw the seams of that ball as I reached up for it with my right hand as it approached me, fully expecting to catch it. But the fellow next to me on my right had similar plans. He put out his left hand in front of mine and the ball caromed off his hand several seats behind us where a mad scramble for the ball ensued. I was excited to have come so close to catching a home-run ball. The disappointed fellow next to me was shaking his hand in pain. He left his seat and came back a few innings later with an ice pack on his hand. He said he planned to play softball that evening, but felt he would be unable to. He thought his left thumb was broken.

The next morning's *Philadelphia Inquirer* said it was one of the hardest and longest homeruns ever hit at Veteran Stadium and estimated it would have traveled a record 485 feet if it were unimpeded. And I almost caught it and I was not afraid, but I probably would have gotten a broken hand or finger or worse out of it if it weren't for the guy next to me.

23

Another big treat that the Delaware River provided us kids was the annual boat ride to Soupy Island. (We Polish kids called it "Zoupy Island" because the Polish word for soup was *zupa*.) We called it Zoupy Island because when we poor kids of Port Richmond arrived at the amusement park, we were provided with a lunch of terrible-tasting soup and crackers. But we didn't care about the soup; our mothers often provided us with a lunch and some money to buy food at the amusement park called the Riverview Amusement Park, located about 5 miles south of Philadelphia on the Jersey side, now long gone. The hour-long ride on the triple-decker, 200-foot long boat was a treat, a thrill for us deprived kids of the inner city. The amusement park was equally exciting. Everything, except the food, was free: the swimming pool, the rides, the games. At 4:00 P.M. the loud horn of the boat could be heard throughout the park. It was time to go home. It was a day we all looked forward to and long remembered.

24

The "Zoupy Island Boat" on its way south to the Riverview Amusement Park slowly sailed under the massive, 6-lane Delaware River Bridge (now called the Benjamin Franklin Bridge), and we craned our necks upward as it did so. So did the El go under the Delaware River Bridge as it careened to the subway section under center Philadelphia on its way to 69th Street. So we were familiar with the underside of the bridge. We were curious to see what it was like to see the topside of the bridge. Six of us decided to walk to the bridge and over the bridge to Camden, New Jersey, at that time a thriving metropolis, but, today, a shattered, slum-strewn, bankrupt, corrupt city. The walk was longer than we expected. We walked south down Richmond Street to Delaware Avenue and its docks and piers and busy market places. When arrived at the base of the bridge, we craned our necks upward and we were dwarfed by its immensity. We walked west a few blocks to 4th Street to the entrance of the bridge. We then walked over the bridge, pausing in the middle, to watch boats glide by below us. We saw an extension of the El taking commuters to Camden whiz by. We then walked around the city of Camden as though we were in a foreign country. We then turned around to head back home by retracing our steps. We were tired, hungry, thirsty. As we were walking past one of the markets on Delaware Avenue, Beebo got the idea of swiping a watermelon from a horse drawn wagon that was left unattended. Two of us carried the watermelon quickly from the market place and by the time the peddler came out of the market to his wagon, we were long gone. Anyway, he didn't miss it. Two of us at a time took turns carrying the 30-pound watermelon, which we didn't mind doing because we looked at the watermelon with anticipatory glee. We couldn't wait until we got to Port Richmond to cut it up and eat it. It certainly would slake our thirst. We continued taking turns, two at a time, carrying it. Our turns became shorter as the watermelon grew heavier but we carried on. We were nearing home; we were at Richmond and Somerset Streets, just a few blocks more and we would enjoy this luscious watermelon. But it grew heavier and it became increasingly awkward the heavier the watermelon became to carry it between us as we walked sideways. It was Beerzy's and my turn to carry it for the next block. It was easier to carry the watermelon if we walked in a single file. The only problem was that the lead person had to walk backwards; obviously, he couldn't see behind him. Beerzy bumped into a fire hydrant, stumbled, dropped his end of the watermelon. It fell to the ground breaking into many different pieces. We looked down at the shattered watermelon in disbelief. After carrying it for several miles, we dropped it just as we were nearing home. I think I was not the only one with the thought, "God punished us for swiping the watermelon from that poor peddler."

25

After that somewhat lengthy interlude, I return to my errand to Radzikowski's store, as I bound over the steps of the residents of Mercer Street. Next to the Murawokie lived a secretive German immigrant couple that nobody knew much about, except that they frequently fought. One summer evening their domestic quarrel spilled outdoors, attracting a crowd of neighbors who were always looking to watch a good quarrel, if not a fight. But the man was so enraged by the crowd he forgot his wife and turned his anger on the crowd. He ran back into the house and emerged with a sword, waving it menacingly at us. The crowd became silent and backed off. When he took a step towards the crowd, we all started running towards our homes. My oldest brother Joe snatched me into his arms and ran the 60 feet to our home, where the open door was waiting for us. Joe threw me into the house and slammed the door behind him. We heard a thud on the door. The next morning a chip was off the ledge of the door. Joe told me the nick was caused by the sword last night. I believe(d) him.

26

The Crawfords lived next door to the German immigrants. The Crawfords were another strange yet elegant family by our standards. I say elegant because their home was newly brick-pointed. They had a wooden awning over the front window, a fancy glass front door, and a late-model car. They also had a retarded fortyish daughter, Louise, who seemed to be chewing on something all the time. We later found out it was her tongue. She was barely understandable when she talked. She mumbled a lot and foamed at the mouth a little when she spoke. She wore round rimless glasses, a cotton cap and sweater, even during the hottest days of summer. She wore saddle shoes that seemed to point in opposite directions when she walked.

The Crawfords had a grown son, Willie, who seemed a nice enough guy. The parents were nice and respectable, even elegant by our standards, as I said. So I was shocked when Willie was engaged in a fistfight with next door neighbor Johnny "Mad Dog" Madden. Mrs. Crawford, from the front steps and above the din of the crowd, hollered at Willie when he was being beaten badly, "Kick him in the balls, Willie! Kick him in the balls!" Maybe Willie should have heeded his mother's advice and resorted to kickboxing because Mad Dog, using the common parlance of the day, "kicked the shit outa' Willie."

Then over the Pijanowski's step with their beautiful blond buxom daughter, Mania (Polish for Mary), for whom I had a secret crush all through grade school and high school until I left for the seminary. (I did muster enough courage to take her to the Richmond Movies and I did put my arm around her and placed my hand on her breast, and she did politely remove my hand, because she was a good girl.) She went to Nazareth Academy, an expensive Catholic girls academy in Torresdale, an affluent neighborhood several miles north of Port Richmond.

Many years later after I left the priesthood, my wife and I, while visiting my niece Lucy at the homestead on Mercer Street, bumped into Mania and her second husband at the parish bazaar. She was still youthful, attractive but a little heavier, a little more subdued. She invited us for a drink at their home on Miller Street, a few blocks away. What a magnificent tiny row house on a dismally dark street! Her second husband Frank was handy. (I never liked her first husband, Tommy. I never thought their marriage would last.) He gutted and rebuilt the entire interior. He put in cathedral ceilings, a powder room between the living room and kitchen. He put in a huge mirror that covered the entire length of the living room, which gave the illusion of doubling the size of the living room. The thick, fluffy carpet was white; the new, expensive furniture was white, laced with gold curlicues. Perhaps all a bit garish. But the location of the house was poor. Facing them across the narrow street, the width of Mercer Street, was the massive red-stoned sidewall of the Romanesque Nativity of the Blessed Virgin Mary Church, the Irish church. I don't think the people living on Miller Street ever saw sunlight from their front windows.

After a few beers I confessed my youthful infatuation with Mania. "Ever since grammar school I had a crush on you." "Now's a good time to tell me, you jerk. It's a little late isn't it? I had a crush on you too." (Her husband, Frank, a bit insecure, was visibly displeased. My wife, more secure, didn't seem to mind.) Mania told us she hadn't worked in a few years because of a bad heart. I never thought it would be the last time I would see Mania. My niece informed me she died a few months later.

Then, ever forward to the Radzikowskis, onto and over the Majkas, friends of my parents who visited us occasionally, and their two uppity daughters, Ida and Florence, whom my older brothers dated on occasion, and a son, Junior, a body-building fanatic, who rented a garage across the street and converted it into a weight-lifting gym. He got me interested in weight lifting. Then a final 50-foot sprint across Madison Street to the Radzikowski store. It never occurred to

Ed Chrzanowski

me what might have happened if someone had stepped out of his or her home as I was leaping over their front steps. Luckily, nobody ever did.

130

27

Mr. & Mrs. Radzikowski were nice elderly people, older than my parents. The store was formerly a private home. The Radzikowskis knocked out the front wall and put in a display window and they knocked out the wall between their living and dining rooms. They and their daughter lived in the kitchen behind the store and on the second floor above the store. The store was a busy store, not only with every inch of wall space filled with groceries, but often every inch of floor space filled with people. Never had I been in that small, narrow store when it was not crowded. At the far end was the butcher block where Mr. Radzikowski butchered and packaged the fresh meats. At the other end near the entrance was the customers' check out-counter where Mrs. Radzikowski weighed and tabulated the cost, with a long display freezer filled with fresh and processed meats between them. And it was a good thing they had this freezer between them because the Radzikowskis frequently argued openly, particularly when by late afternoon Mr. Radzikowski had been in his cups. In front of the refrigerator were huge wooden tubs of pickled cucumbers, pickled green tomatoes, pickled herrings floating in a dark vinaigrette dressing. To keep down the dust from the foot traffic, sawdust mixed with an oily solution was liberally strewn all over the floor.

Mrs. Radzikowski often waited on me ahead of others because I always came for one or two items that Mom forgot. I'd tell, in Polish, of course, Mrs. Radzikowski what my mother wanted and I'd hand her a small account book. She'd give me the item and in large bold numbers mark the cost of the item in the book. I then bounded home again. (For variety's sake, I would have bounded over the steps of the houses on the opposite side of the street, but there were no houses. The other side of the street consisted of a huge three-story truck storage and truck and auto repair garage and about 20 individual car garages, owned by Mr. Furtek.)

This smallish green-covered account book was very important to us and to all the households that dealt with the Radzikowskis. This was my parents' way of buying food on account. Every Friday evening when Pop came home from work with his paycheck, Mom and he would pore over that book for hours: counting and checking and double-checking. They would wonder what item was bought that could have cost that much. Were they overcharged? Did somebody make a mistake? They would complain about this or that extravagance, and then the moment of truth: Would Pop's paycheck cover the amount? Often, it did not. The Radzikowskis, after checking Mom and Pop's figures, would then give us extra time to pay, and it would be time to economize for a week or two to do so.

Our fare was simple even when we weren't economizing. Bread and butter for breakfast, a bologna sandwich for lunch, and maybe a TastyKake or TastyPie for a snack, if Mom could afford them. When Pop worked days, his breakfast consisted of a glass of milk mixed with a fresh egg. During the week for supper, we often had a huge bowl of potatoes, mixed with sauerkraut and small pieces of *skwarki*, crisp-fried fat back, interspersed for flavoring, for which we all searched with our forks because that was often our only meat for the evening. We had either beet soup, or cabbage soup, or a sorrel soup, all mixed generously with boiled potatoes. The beet soup was our favorite. It was always served hot, always with a lot of beets and potatoes, and a healthy dash of vinegar. I suppose if Mom served it cold and with sour cream we would be having a delicacy.

Often, on Friday we had fried fish. I watched my mother run the fish through a bowl of raw eggs, then sprinkle the fish with flour and sometimes with homemade breadcrumbs. The only problem with the fish was that it wasn't filleted properly, and we were always feeling for bones in our mouth with our tongue before we swallowed. Often we had to eat a slice of bread to catch the bone before it got lodged in our throats. Sometimes, we had potato pancakes on Friday.

Sometimes, we had *kiszka,* a sausage of barley grain, encased in an intestine. My father enjoyed his *kiszka,* although we were not fond of it, and would have had it every Friday except my mother said the encasement constituted meat, and it violated the Catholic Friday meat abstinence rule. My father said it did not but my mother claimed she asked the priest in confession and he said it did.

My father had his own pre-supper ritual when he worked the day shift. He came home promptly at 4:30, already showered at work where he took care of furnaces that burned coal for the natural gases in the coal. (A by-product of this procedure was coke— coal with the gas burned off. It, too, was used to heat residences, but it couldn't compete with coal because coal was longer lasting. We were one of the few in our neighborhood who used coke in our home because my father received a discount. The name of the company was Kopper's Coke, on Richmond Street in Bridesburg, long out of business.) At one end of the kitchen table, he sat in a bulky, second-hand, leather, rocking chair, opened his daily Polish newspaper, the *Nowy Swiat*, "The New World." My mother poured him a bottle of Ortlieb's Beer and served him a dish of *sledzi*, fresh herring piled high with marinated onions, or just a fresh salad loaded with onions and a vinegar and oil dressing.

Almost daily, as my father was having his beer and herring, I sidled up to him and asked him for a penny to buy some chocolate at Labus's Candy Store, next to Furtek's on Allegheny Avenue. Sometimes he gave me the penny, sometimes he didn't, depending on his mood, but he always pulled my sideburns, a sign of his affection, I suppose, which almost made me cry with pain. But the penny was worth the pain, I figured. When Pop finished his Happy Hour, Mom would summon us to the dinner table to begin dinner.

The weekend menu was much better. Practically every Saturday, unless we couldn't afford it, supper consisted of thin slices of tough roast beef, cooked in a light watery gravy, loaded with onions, that we soaked up with several slices of rye bread slathered in butter.

When I look back at those Saturday meals, I think we were conned. We thought we were having roast beef for supper, and we were to a certain small extent, but actually it was more like a rye bread soaked in watery gravy meal.

Sundays was a feast. For breakfast, we had a mixture of donuts, cheese cake, apple cake, and crumb cake from Kolecki's Bakery on Madison Avenue, a few houses from Radzikowskis, which, unlike most stores, was in the middle of the block and not at the corner. Kolecki's Bakery was a converted double home, with the wall between the two homes removed to form a wide store, the width of two houses, with the actual bakery behind the store. The Koleckis and their two sons and three beautiful daughters all lived on the second floor. What amazed me then and now was how very lean the Koleckis were, despite owning a bakery and having all those pastries at their disposal. Mr. Kolecki, who baked but sometimes waited on customers when busy, especially Sunday morning after church, was about 6 feet tall, thin, with rimless glasses, a slight Hitler mustache, a tall baker's hat on his balding head and a white apron covered with flour. His elegant wife was also tall and thin and so were their three blond daughters who, surprisingly, never seemed to work at the business. One boy, again tall and thin, drove the delivery truck; the other boy, tall and thin, was killed in an automobile accident, I believe.

Sunday mornings, after all the Masses, the bakery was packed with people coming from church. The bakery was also busy every night at 8:00 when the bread for the following morning was baked. Mom would give me a quarter and tell me to hurry to get a loaf of *razowy chleb,* rye bread. I really bounded over those steps, to and fro, to get the bread home while it was still hot. Mom then would cut herself and me a thick slice and slather a generous amount of butter on it. It was so good. That would often be our bedtime snack.

On Sundays for dinner, at 3:00 in the afternoon, Mom started us off with a big dish of homemade chicken soup with either noodles or boiled potatoes, garnished with carrots and parsley. Then came the boiled chicken, mashed potatoes and a vegetable.

Once in a while for a diversion, Mom prepared duck for the Sunday dinner. On Saturday morning, she bought the live duck at Maxie Shapiro's, who was located just a few doors away. I watched from the kitchen window as she took the duck to the backyard and held the quacking duck between her knees. She then bent the duck's neck forward, slit the throat, and drained the duck's blood into a pail for the next ten minutes. Saturday night, she boiled the duck, pulled out the feathers and singed the duck over the kitchen stove to remove the last of the feathers. This last process produced an odor I found very unpleasant. Next day, she cooked the duck and made duck's soup out of the blood, mixed with vinegar and potatoes, a delicacy for all of us, except Joe, who could not even look at duck's blood soup. Joe ate something else after we finished our dinner of duck and duck's blood. Here in the Buffalo area where I settled after I left the priesthood, Poles prepare their *czarnina* (actually means black) with prunes and prefer a sweetened soup while we in Philadelphia preferred a vinegary, tart flavor.

Lent was a somber season for us. Mom would make our meals even plainer than usual. We all gave something up for Lent. Even Pop gave up his beer and weekend binges for Lent. I gave up my penny candy treat before supper. So we were glad when the end of Lent approached. In addition to preparing spiritually for Our Lord's Resurrection by participating as much as we could in the church's rich liturgy of Holy Week, we prepared to celebrate physically and materially the end of Lent and the coming of spring. Mom would buy ham, two kinds of *kielbasa*—smoked and fresh; butter in the form of a lamb, several loaves of rye bread; she would boil dozens of eggs and because of lack of time, she would color them all a drab brown by boiling them in onion peels. She would bake mounds of *chruszcziki*, a delicate doughy pastry sprinkled with sugar, often called bow-ties in this country, and a *babka*, a bread-like pastry strewn with raisins, excellent when fresh and covered with butter. Pop would buy several cases of beer and a few bottles of whiskey for guests, so Pop would say but Mom knew better. And we would have guests all day Easter Sunday and Easter Monday or *Dyngus* Day, when the boys sprinkled the girls with water and the girls gently slapped the boys on the back with pussy willows, an old Polish courting ritual.

The Christmas Vigil meal, *Wigilja* in Polish, was also a solemn, beautiful meal. The meal was a simple, meatless meal, consisting of several types of fish, but it was the simple ceremony that preceded the meal that made it so special. All of us had to be present for this meal, without exception, no matter how old you were. All of us standing around the kitchen table, Pop would delicately take out of a plastic envelope the *Oplatek,* an ornately embossed thin piece of unleavened bread. He broke off a small piece for himself, handed us all a small piece, beginning with Mom, then Joe, etc. He wished us all good health, prosperity for the coming year, and apologized for his shortcomings. He then hugged and kissed Mom (I almost fainted the first time.). We all ate our piece of the *Oplatek*. Then Mom would do the same and then Joe, etc. Even I, the youngest got my turn. Poor Stan stuttered when he spoke Polish and when he was nervous. He began to stutter and I began to laugh until Pop lightly hit me on the head. This was a solemn occasion—no laughing. There was enough hugging and kissing and well-wishing and apologizing that night to last a year—and it did. It was beautiful while it lasted. I think the Poles are blessed to have these traditions, but I understand they are slowly fading away.

28

As I got older and Joe was old enough to work where Pop worked, our menu became better, more diversified. We had meat practically every evening: Polish sausage (*kielbasa*) and sauerkraut, thin fried pork chops smothered with fried onions, hamburgers and meatloaf, the best I have ever tasted even though they were prepared with more stale bread than ground meat. Once in a while, Mom made *pierogis* (dough patties filled with potatoes, cheese, or sauerkraut), *golambkis* (cabbage rolls), and *chruszczik*i, bowties, a pastry. The *pierogis, golambkis and chruczcziki* were delicious, but I found out later when I ate at other people's homes or restaurants, the cabbage leaves of the *golambki* were too big, too thick with little of the meat-filling. The same was true of the *pierogi;* there was too much dough and not enough of the filling. The *chruszcziki* were also thick and heavy, unlike the thin, delicate *chruszczcziki* I've eaten elsewhere. But this was done probably by design by Mom. They were more filling, more economical to prepare them that way.

At Easter time, Mom, as I said, made a huge bread, about two feet by four feet, weighing about 20 pounds, with a liberal amount of raisins in it. This was Mom's version of the Polish *placek*. Covered with slabs of butter, it was delicious, the first week or so after it was baked. But when it hardened it wasn't so good. Even dipping it into coffee couldn't soften it, but we still ate it until it was all gone. It was our daily breakfast fare for weeks after Easter.

When we were behind in our account at the Radzikowskis, to avoid embarrassment, my mother sometimes had me go to Majeski's Delicatessen on Allegheny Avenue. This, too, was a converted private residence but probably three times the size of Radzikowkis with not nearly a quarter of the inventory, and there never was a time when more than two people were there when I entered and I think I knew why. His quarter pound of lunchmeat was about half the weight of Radzikowski's. Although I could never see him, I was too short, even at that early age, I suspected he held his thumb on the scale or had a different measurement altogether. Every time he handed me the lunchmeat, he would say in accented English: "That will be 25 cents, Edziu. But because you are my *very* best customer, I am going to do you a favor. I am going to charge you only (then a long pause during which I held my breath expectantly) 25 cents." Even at the hundredth or so time, I was still hoping that he would knock off a nickel or a penny, but he never did and I never stopped hoping he would—he was so convincing or I was so gullible.

29

We who lived on the narrow north-south side streets off Allegheny Avenue that ran east and west regarded the residents of Allegheny Avenue as wealthier, as of a higher, ritzier class. Allegheny Avenue was and still is one of the leading east-west arteries of North Philadelphia or maybe of all Philadelphia. It spans the entire east-west width of the city—from the Delaware River on the east to the Schuylkill River on the west, a distance of about 10 miles, or about an hour's ride on the 60 trolley car. And it is wide, broad, about half as broad as the famous Broad Street, the main north-south artery of the city that divides the entire city into east and west and under which the Broad Street Subway travels.

Allegheny Avenue was the hub of our existence. That was where most of the doctors and lawyers had their offices, where many businesses were, where the park was, where the three leading Roman Catholic churches, Polish, Irish, German, were within a few blocks of each other, where the funeral parlors were, where the banks were, where the few restaurants were and, and where most of the bars were, practically one on every other corner.

The intersection of Mercer Street where we lived and Allegheny Avenue was the hub of our activities, and I was fortunate to have lived a few short yards from there. As youngsters, it seemed we had everything we needed then at the corner of Mercer and Allegheny. We had the protection from the elements of cold, wintry nights in the doorway of Furtek's Dry Goods store, passing around a cigarette that we purchased for a penny at Labus' candy store next door, while listening to Googoo's stories of Left-to-the-Right Boom, whose Superman-like hero was able to defeat his adversaries by elongating his left and right arms at will, and of Leppee, a ghoul-like character that nightly scared the hell out of us. On nice nights, we sat on the doorstep of Furtek's daughter's beauty parlor next door just a few feet away from the dry goods store. For a change, we would congregate on Maxie's produce store steps, on the other side of Mercer Street. But we were reluctant to do that because his steps were not always clean and a stench came from under the doors of his produce store.

During the day, Mercer and Allegheny was also our favorite hangout. We played wire ball, hand ball, half ball, tire ball, and two-hand touch football there. There were two wooden utility poles about 50 feet apart on Furtek's property. A heavy electrical wire spanned the two poles. Mr. Furtek's home's side wall served as an excellent backdrop. It had no windows near the front part of his home where the dry goods store was. It was ideal for wire ball. Somebody always seemed to come up with a rubber ball, hollow inside, and small bumps on the outside that we called a pimple ball, for obvious reasons. The object of wire ball was to stand on Maxie's pavement across from Furtek's pavement and to try to hit the wire. If you missed the wire, the ball would come back and most likely be caught. When it was caught three times, the opponent took over throwing the ball at the wire. If you hit the wire and the ball was deflected and not caught, which was likely, you gained a point. Eleven points was the game. We played this game hours on end until the ball developed a crack because of wear or Mr. Furtek, annoyed by the incessant pounding of the ball against his wall, would chase us away, only for us to resume the game five minutes later.

When the ball developed a crack, we would tear it apart into two equal halves and then play half ball with the two halves. Somebody would provide a sawed-off broom handle as the bat. The pitcher would float a half-ball to the batter who flailed away at the elusive object. It was extremely difficult to hit the half-ball thrown overhand because it floated in evenly, parallel to the ground, giving only about a quarter-inch of surface to hit. Only Beebo was able to hit the half-ball pitched overhand with any regularity.

We played a game we called handball. With an intact pimple ball, a batter would throw it in the air with his left hand, much like a tennis player serving, and hit the ball with his right hand. In this game we had fielders strewn along Mercer Street all the way to the other side of Allegheny Avenue, especially when Beebo or Googoo or Booj were at bat. It was not unusual for a fielder to dodge traffic, to stop traffic, to stop the 60 trolley car on Allegheny Avenue, as he circled under the ball.

Beebo was uncanny in these games. In wire ball, he hit the wire two out of three times while we were lucky to hit the wire once out of three. In half ball, we couldn't hit the half ball if it was thrown overhand but Beebo could. Routinely, he would smack the half-ball out into the middle of Allegheny Avenue. In hand ball he was the only one who could hit the ball to the other side of Allegheny Avenue, sometimes hitting the window of the Royal Café. He had fielders scurrying all over Allegheny Avenue trying to catch his long, high handballs.

We also played two-hand touch football on Mercer Street, sometimes with a real-live football but more often with a clump of newspapers, tightly bound with several thick rubber bands or bands from cut-up inner tubes. We passed with this makeshift football, we ran with it, using those two wooden poles about 50 feet apart on Furtek's property that were previously mentioned as goal lines.

We played marbles in the street gutters until our knuckles were raw, trying to hit our opponent's marble ahead of us, and if we did, we took possession of it. We sometimes played hopscotch and jumped rope and played jacks with the girls. We skated up and down Mercer Street until the skates, fastened by clamps tightened by skate keys on to the soles of our shoes, tore the soles off our shoes, or the skates were so worn down that the wheels developed holes and cracks in them and would not turn easily and smoothly anymore. Then we used the worn-out skates for our pushcart scooters, made out of an empty upright wooden produce box (usually from Maxie's) with a board, nailed to and extending from the bottom of the box to stand on and to propel yourself, just like today's aluminum scooter. But we didn't pay $59.95 for our wooden scooters.

We played "Buck-Buck." We divided into two teams of usually six or seven to a team. One person stood against the wall. The remaining members of the team bent over holding on to the waist of the teammate ahead of him. The opposing team, one at a time, hollered, "Buck buck, here I come," and jump as high and as far ahead as he could on to the backs, shoulders, and sometimes heads of those bent over. The object of the game was to get everybody on to the backs of the bent over team and to have that team cave in at some point. If the team did cave in, the jumping team would then repeat the process. If the team did not cave in, the roles were reversed. Another wrinkle to the game that we sometimes observed was that the members of the team on the backs of the other team were not allowed to show their teeth. The team member standing against the wall would try his best to get someone to show his teeth. If he succeeded, the teams exchanged places even if the team did not cave in.

We also gambled a lot. We threw pennies against a wall or towards a crack in the pavement. Whoever's penny came closest to the wall or to the crack won all the pennies. We flipped baseball cards that served as a backing to the bubble gum we really purchased. (How we wish we had those baseball cards today!). If you matched your opponent's flip, the picture of the player was heads and the other statistical side was tales, you won all the cards flipped; if you did not, your opponent won all the cards. We flipped pennies, heads or tales. Like with cards, if you matched your opponent's flip, you won; if not, you lost. If we had the playing cards and enough guys with enough pennies, we had spontaneous penny ante card games on somebody's doorstep, unlike Sunday morning games which were for higher stakes and played in the center of the street. At Easter time, we even gambled with decorated hard-boiled eggs. On Easter Sunday we would run out of the house, hollering, "Epper! Epper!" I have no idea what that meant, other than it was a challenge to anyone who wanted to match the hardness of his egg against yours. If somebody came forward to accept the challenge, you held your egg by encircling it with your thumb and forefinger near the tip, allowing just enough surface of your egg to be tapped by the tip of your opponent's egg. Whoever's egg cracked first was the loser and the winner would take the slightly cracked egg and usually ate it right then and there, without salt. Some would prepare for Epper a year in advance. They would bury an egg in the ground at Easter time and dig it up the following year. These eggs were hard as a rock, but these illegal eggs were soon found out. If they easily cracked three or four eggs, they would be declared illegal and nobody would Epper with an unethical individual with such an egg.

30

A summer event that we all looked forward to was the annual parish bazaar. People flocked to the schoolyard and to the parish hall. There were all kinds of games of chance and all kinds of food to eat. It was a time to see and talk to the Sisters as they rocked on the back porch of the convent, watching the festivities. And there were amusement rides. I recall Beebo and I took the Ferris wheel ride. I was afraid of heights to begin with, and Beebo just aggravated the situation by rocking the bench-like ride, with just a horizontal rod in front of us to keep us in, almost to the point of flipping over. I pleaded with Beebo to stop. The more I pleaded, the more he rocked to the point that, especially at the top of the arc when we could see the lights of the Delaware River Bridge about ten miles south, all I saw were our legs silhouetted against the moon. To this day, I will not go on a Ferris wheel ride that is not enclosed. Now my wife taunts me about my cowardice. She doesn't realize what I went through with Beebo and the Ferris wheel at the parish bazaar.

31

All of the above were summer activities. We were limited as to what we could do in the winter. We had no ice skates, no skating rinks, no skis, no toboggans, but a few did have sleds. When it snowed, we would go to Almond Street Hill between Madison and Westmoreland Streets, a block west of Mercer Street, to sled. It was and is probably the only street in Port Richmond streets that had some significant decline to it. A sledder would run about ten feet from the top of the hill at Madison Street with sled in front of him and then belly flop on the sled for the rest of the ride down the hill. Sometimes he would allow his friends, who did not own a sled (and there were many), to take turns belly flopping on top of him as he slid by.

Sleds have a warm spot in my heart because a sled is the first and only toy my father ever bought me. I was just wild with delight when I saw him carrying home that new, sparkling sled the day before Christmas. (Remarkably, yesterday for the first time

157

since I was 10 years old, at a local hardware store, I saw a sled like the one my father bought me. Only the price was $59.95. I'm sure my father didn't pay that much.) Every year I was so disappointed, and my parents saw the disappointment on my face, I'm sure, to find only a few new clothes, the same Nativity scene, the same empty, nicely wrapped boxes under the Christmas tree, but no toys. Maybe it was the disappointment written all over my face that prompted my father to buy me this sled that was almost as tall as I was and that you could actually maneuver a little by pulling on the cross-bar at the top of the sled.

One evening, a few weeks later, when it snowed, I told my mother I was going to Almond Street to sled. Instead, I was sidetracked by my buddies. "Let's do something really dangerous. Let's go to Allegheny Avenue and hitch rides on to cars," said Beerzy. The comparatively slow sled ride down Almond Street Hill was too tame for my friends and me. With some trepidation, I agreed. We hid between parked cars on Allegheny Avenue and waited for slow-moving cars with chains on their tires to approach us. We would run out from between the cars, run after the car with sled in hand, place the sled down with Beerzy on top of me and grab the back bumper of the car. We held our arms out straight and rigid, in case the car stopped abruptly so we wouldn't slide under the car. We enjoyed the ride for a couple of blocks until the driver got wise to the cause of his car's sluggish performance, stopped the car and chased us away.

Some drivers knew we were hitching a ride and rather than stop the car to chase us off they tried to get rid of us by going faster and by turning side to side and fishtailing down Allegheny Avenue. This made the ride all the more daring for us. We held on for dear life, for if we let go we didn't know where we would end up: into parked cars, into oncoming traffic, into the car itself. We knew it was dangerous but it was fun, especially when the car began to fishtail, hoping to dislodge us, with our legs flapping from side to side, sometimes touching parked cars, almost touching cars coming in the opposite direction, and there was the ever-present danger of the car stopping abruptly and we hitting the bumper with our heads, or worse, ending up underneath the car.

Corpo appeared with his sled on his way to the Almond Street Hill. Seeing how much fun we were having, he decided to join us. With Sajo as his partner, we waited for a double-parked car on Allegheny Avenue to soon take off. The driver came out of Sitko's Pharmacy, got in the car and we hooked on the back of the car. The four of us were ready for a great joy ride down Allegheny Avenue all the way to Belgrade Street if not further. The driver put the car in gear; the engine roared but the car would not move. He gave the car more gas; still the car would not move. All it was doing was slipping and sliding and throwing smelly fumes and smoke from its muffler and dirty snow and ice from its chained tires in our faces. We decided we had enough of this. We let go of the back bumper, got up and started walking away. Just then the driver gunned the motor again and the unhindered car took off like a race car and the astonished driver almost hit the car about 30 feet ahead of him. The driver got out of the car and went to the back of the car to see what was wrong with the car. He must have figured out the problem when he saw the four of us running down Allegheny Avenue.

I just did this car-hopping only once because I realized how dangerous it was afterwards. But kids are still doing it in Philadelphia and elsewhere 60 years later. In Philly, they still call it "hopping cars" and "bumper-hitching." In Detroit they call it "shagging." On the Eastern Seaboard, they call it "skitching" and in northern Indiana," hooky-bobbing." A recent Associated Press newspaper article out of Philadelphia reported that today's kids are hitching rides on to cars without sleds, just squatting down, grabbing the bumper and using their shoes as skis. Others, flat on their bellies, use their entire body as a ski or a sled. We, at least, used sleds. After reporting several deaths and accidents, one in Bristol, a northern suburb of Philadelphia, the article concluded with a quote from a Mike Acobacey from Northeast Philadelphia where hopping cars is still a pastime: "They've done it since there were horse and buggies. They'll be doing it for the rest of your life and longer." I don't know whether they did it in the horse and buggy days, but we did it in our time, 60 years ago.

Our other winter activities were not so dangerous or exciting. We did the usual things. We had snowball fights, although some fought dirty and threw iceballs, a piece of ice inside a snowball, which could be dangerous if you were hit in the face; we built snowmen and washed girls' faces with snow. We carefully developed a patch of hard snow into an ice slide and then we ran on the snow until we got to the ice slide, one foot behind the other and in a crouching position, and let ourselves rip for the length of the slide, 20, 30, 40 feet. We fought and wrestled to gain possession of the top of a mound of snow and called the game, "King of the Hill." When there was no snow on the ground, we sometimes stole a few potatoes from Maxie's during the day and that evening built a bonfire outside his store with his discarded cardboard and wooden boxes. We kept ourselves warm and at the same time enjoyed baked potatoes, compliments of Maxie, but without salt and butter and often with the center of the potato still raw. The fire would not last long enough to bake the entire potato. To keep the bonfire going longer, new arrivals to the bonfire were told to "chip or skip." Contribute to the fire or move on.

32

The older we got the more the 60 trolley car was our link to the world outside of Port Richmond. The 60 traveled east and west, the full width of Philadelphia, from the east from the car barn at Richmond Street and Allegheny Avenue to the west, to 30th Street and Allegheny Avenue, a few streets before you entered Fairmount Park, the zoo, and the Schuylkill River. The 60 trolley car was powered electrically by a metallic electrical pole extending from the roof of the trolley car to overhead electrical lines that extended the full length of the trolley line. There were two poles, one on each end of the trolley and two sets of controls, one on each end. When the trolley car reached the end of the line, one electrical line was lowered and the other extended upward and a lever controlling the trolley was taken from one end of the trolley car to the other end. These double sets of controls and power lines were necessary because there was no turnaround at the 30th Street end of the line.

The trolley car could accommodate about 50 seated passengers and about 80 passengers sitting and standing. It was manned by a motorman and a conductor, both dressed in dark trousers and matching jackets and railway caps. The conductor stood near the back door through which everybody entered. He had a money collector and dispenser fastened on his belt and a hole puncher with which he punched the time the transfer was still good to use. They used different colored transfers every day. The fare was ten cents which included a free transfer to another public transportation system, which was usually the elevated-subway train at Kensington and Allegheny Avenues. The elevated train went north about five miles to the Bridge Street Station, the northern end of the line, and south about 20 miles to the 69th Street Station, the Southwestern end of the line.

I was intrigued by the motorman of the 60 trolley. I would sit near the front of the trolley and watch how he turned a lever to the left several times and slightly to the right to get the trolley moving and a little back to the right to slow down the trolley and how he turned the lever to the left several times and a little to the right to get the trolley going again, which never seemed to go more than 15-20 miles an hour, stopping every hundred yards or so to collect and dispense passengers. I enjoyed when the motorman clanged the bell by pulling on the chain above him to warn motorists and pedestrians to get out of the way and he had a cowcatcher as well, which we once tested, to see if it really worked.

It was approaching darkness one summer evening. Beerzy and I were bored; we wanted a new adventure. We dug a huge rock out of the park, carried it across Allegheny Avenue near the corner of Almond Street and waited between two parked cars for the eastbound 60 to come. When the 60 trolley was at Belgrade Street, a block away, we quickly ran out from between the cars and placed the rock on the tracks and returned to our hiding place between the cars where we waited to see what would happen. By now it was dark. The motorman didn't see the rock. The trolley hit the rock, made a crushing sound and pushed it forward about ten feet beyond where we were hiding. The terribly annoyed motorman stopped the trolley, cursing under his breath, got out and carried the rock back to the sidewalk near where we were hiding. He looked around for the perpetrators, but Beerzy and I, now frightened at what we did, bent lower between the cars and literally held our breath until the motorman got back into the trolley. We never tried this prank again because we found out that the cowcatcher did work and it was too risky with possible grave consequences.

Back then, on Sundays, the PRT (Philadelphia Rapid Transit) allowed an adult to take two children under twelve, supposedly his own, free on any public transportation vehicle. On Sunday afternoon, two, four, sometimes six of us would stand, like orphans, at the corner of Thompson and Allegheny Avenue and ask adults: "Will you please be our father for today?" and most would say yes because it didn't cost them anything. Then we would have the audacity to ask them to ask for a transfer for us.

We would get off the 60 trolley at K&A (Kensington and Allegheny), run diagonally across Kensington Avenue, race up the four flights of stairs to the southbound Allegheny Station. We would take three or four steps at a time, holding our breath as we were doing so, trying not to inhale the stench of urine of Saturday night revelers, puddled at every landing.

When we boarded the train, commonly and affectionately known as "the El," we would run through the cars to the front car, slide open the front window and look out at what was to us a glorious sight: what seemed like endless miles of tracks ahead of us. We watched the train tracks quickly disappear beneath us as the El gained speed; we felt the wind against our faces, giving us the illusion of more speed than the 30 or 40 miles per hour it actually was going; we heard the clackety-clack sound of the wheels over the railjoints; we watched the dilapidated buildings on both sides of the tracks recede behind us; we tried to identify the various churches in the distance; we looked up at the massive structure of the Delaware

River Bridge as we rumbled under it. We heard the ear-splitting screeching sound of the wheels as the train slowed down to almost a halt, and turned sharply to the right and headed gradually downward to transform itself into a subway at the Second Street Station. We were plunged into almost total darkness for about 20 minutes, except when the subway approached a station. We emerged again into daylight and changed from subway to El again at the 37th Street station and remained so until we arrived at the end of the line, the 69th Street station.

We ran down the steps of the train station (not reeking with urine because this was a better part of the city) to the Upper Darby section of Philadelphia. For us, Upper Darby, West Philadelphia, was a different world from our Port Richmond in Northeast Philadelphia. There were no longer row houses, narrow treeless streets, corner stores, rowdy corner bars, staggering drunks, noisy trolley lines, card games being played in the middle of the street, no cops walking their beat, no patrol cars patrolling the neighborhood, no kids playing wire-ball, half-ball, hose-ball, or handball in the streets, dodging cars and trolleys on Allegheny Avenue, no kids playing marbles in the park. In fact, there were no parks here. The whole neighborhood was a park to us. Here you had huge homes, mansions that you saw only in the movies, with trees all around them, with no cars parked in the streets, with driveways to single, double, triple garages, housing late-model cars. The tree-lined streets were wide and winding. The homes had flowerbeds all around them, even along the sides and in the back. Their lawns were manicured, front and back. The backyards were spacious. We took off our sneakers and socks just to feel the softness and coolness of the lawns. People were washing their cars, watering their lawns, pruning their flowers. They had backyard pools, backyard grills. Boys and girls and grownups in shorts and bare feet were playing a strange game that involved hitting a small feathered object with small racquets over an elevated net.

Now it was time to return to Port Richmond. This could be a lot dicier than leaving it, for the men of Upper Darby were not so willing to be fathers for a day as the men of Port Richmond were. Often, we had to ask a lot more of them to be our fathers before we got any takers, and as the day wore on, we often got nervous. But that was the chance we took to spend Sunday afternoon visiting this Shangri-La existence by way of a spectacular train ride—at no cost. What a way to spend a Sunday afternoon.

Sometimes we took the 60 beyond K&A. On a fall or wintry Sunday afternoon, using the same father-son tactic, we took the 60 to Broad Street to catch the Broad Street Subway south to the end of the line to the football stadium in South Philly where for a dime, kids under 12 accompanied by an adult, could see the Philadelphia Eagles of the National Football League play. We saw the 5'7" quarterback Davey O'Brien, the Heisman Trophy winner from Texas Christian University, outplay the great Sammy Baugh in a 1940 shootout. We saw the 226-pound fullback Dave

Smuckler, a local boy from Temple University, rush and pass our beloved Eagles to an infrequent victory. We saw the one-eyed quarterback Tommy Thompson valiantly try, but fail to bring our club around.

Sometimes we took the 60 even farther west to 21st Street to watch the Philadelphia Phillies or the Philadelphia A's play major league baseball at Shibe Park at 21st and Lehigh, later named Connie Mack Stadium, after the Philadelphia A's revered owner and manager of many years. The stadium has long since been torn down because it was surrounded by homes which allowed for no parking space and it has been relocated to present Veteran's Stadium at the outskirts of South Philadelphia. We went to the stadium during the week when we couldn't use our father-son ploy, and so we had to pay the ten cents for the 60, if we had it. If we didn't, we walked the three miles to take advantage of the Knothole Gang courtesy, which allowed kids under 12 to free admission to the bleachers. The Knothole Gang was actually started to promote future patronage among the kids and it didn't cost the club anything to allow us to sit in empty bleacher seats. But it was great for us young Philadelphians back then. Instead of lying on the floor in front of the radio and keeping box score of the game as the announcers and sportswriters did and visualize what was going on, we were actually able to see the game for free.

This is when I saw the great Hall of Famer Jimmy Foxx play way after his prime when he was coaxed out of retirement to play during the player shortage years of the war. Although he was in his 40's, way overweight likely from drinking too much, according to the baseball scribes, he could still hit the long ball frequently enough from substandard wartime pitching. But he was too old and over the hill to be our hero. This was when we could sneak down to the grandstand seats late in the game and run out on the field after a game and run the bases, slide into home plate, throw imaginary balls from the pitcher's mound, get close to, and touch our favorite players. This was when I saw the great Joe DiMaggio, in his prime, who with a ripe pulsating carbuncle on his neck and who went 0 for 5 that day, give a kid a good swift kick in the ass with a steel-spiked shoe for jumping up and stealing his cap. From that day on, Joe DiMaggio was no longer my hero. Every time I saw his picture or name in the paper all I could think of was that steel-spiked shoe glistening in the sun and that red, ripe carbuncle pulsating on his neck. When DiMaggio was eulogized as an icon in all the media, I wrote letters to magazines and newspapers describing the ass-kicking scene, but no one would run the letters until a biography came out exposing DiMaggio as a mean-spirited, uncaring, selfish person. Then the local paper published my letter describing the ass-kicking incident.

I took the 60 even farther west to 29th Street, to the stop before the end of the line at 30th Street. On the corner of 29th Street and Allegheny Avenue, was one of the early Howard Johnson restaurants. Next to the restaurant was possibly one of the first underground bowling alleys, the Bowlerdome. Oddly, Mr. Walters managed the restaurant and his wife managed the bowling alley.

Corpo found me the job of setting pins at the bowling alley, but he soon quit to work as a busboy at a downtown restaurant, and I remained for about another year setting pins at the Bowlerdome.

Indeed, the 60 trolley car was our lifeline, our exposure, to the outside world the older we got.

33

I got my start setting pins a few years earlier at the Polish American Social Club at Richmond and Allegheny Avenues, slightly beyond the eastern terminus of the 60 trolley. Actually, it was my first job, arranged by my brother Joe. I was about 12. There were and still are two bowling alleys as you enter the social club. (Back then we called lanes alleys and gutters poodles.) My job and my partner's job was to arrive at the club Monday through Friday at 7:00 P.M., clean the alleys by running a mop up and down the alleys, clean the gutters by doing the same with a different sized mop, dust the rubber mats in the pits from where the bowling pins were set and be ready to set pins for practice at 7:15. The five-man, ten-team league, two different teams each night, usually sponsored by a local bar, began at 7:30. After returning the ball to the bowler, we would grab 2 bowling pins in each hand from the rubber mat in the pit and place our right foot on a treadle under the alley that made ten spikes protrude. We would place the four pins with holes in the bottom on the four spikes on what was designated as pins 1, 3, 6, and 10. We would grab another four pins and place on spikes that were 5 and 9 pins with the left hand and 2 and 4 with the right hand. Finally, we would place the remaining two pins on spikes 7 and 8. We became so adept at this, young as we were, we could practically throw the pins on the spikes, and we could pick up the 16 pound bowling ball quickly with one hand by rolling the ball into the palm of our hand, placing it on the ball return rack, about shoulder high, and give the ball a good spin to return it to the bowler more quickly. Sometimes we spun it so hard that we spun the ball right off the rack and we would have to come out of our pit to retrieve the ball.

For a league match we set 15 games each; we were paid 75 cents for about two hours work, depending on how good the bowlers were and how many strikes the bowlers made. It was grueling work and we thought we were underpaid. There was an elderly man named

Jacek who sat every night by the foul line watching for fouls. By the third game, invariably, he was sound asleep. He was paid 50 cents.

On Saturdays and Sundays there was open bowling. Any member and his guests could bowl for enjoyment or for practice. The price of a game for open bowling was 25 cents, of which the pinsetter received 7 cents and usually a 5-cent tip per game. Many times during open bowling there were lulls, nobody wanted to bowl. To pass the time, I would set pins for my partner and he would do the same for me.

After about a year of this, I had become a pretty good bowler. One Saturday afternoon I recruited Beebo to set pins with me. Beebo was my perennial, personal nemesis, everybody's nemesis. He was the kid who seemed to have preternatural athletic powers, much like Phineas, the leading character of John Knowles's classic novel of the late 50s, *A Separate Peace.* Beebo consistently beat everybody in whatever game or sport we played. I actually recruited him to set pins with me just to challenge him in bowling. Surely,

I thought, I will finally beat Beebo in bowling, for Beebo never put his fingers into a bowling ball, and I had been bowling for nearly a year and had become pretty good at it. Beebo set the pins for me; I bowled a pretty good game in the 160s. I set the next game for Beebo, who, I repeat, never threw a bowling ball before; he simply watched how I did it. He bowled a game in the 190s. It was his matter of fact, smug attitude that infuriated me. "What's so hard about this bowling thing?" he said matter of factly. That was the first and last time I ever recruited Beebo to set pins with me at the Polish American Club.

When I first read Knowles's *A Separate Peace* in the early 1960s and his portrayal of Phineas, the leading character, I immediately thought of the similarities, *mutatis mutandi,* between Phineas and Beebo. I think John Knowles's following descriptions of the 17-year-old Phineas, could be applied to Beebo. "He got away with everything because of the extraordinary kind of person he was. It was quite a compliment to me, as a matter of fact, to have such a person choose me for his best friend." [p. 31, Dell paperback version, 1959] "Finny could shine with everyone, he attracted everyone he met." [p.45] "He rode backward with no hands, he rode on his own handlebars, he jumped off and back on his moving bike as he had seen trick horseback riders do in the movies." [p.53] "He probably thought anything you were good at came without effort. He didn't know yet that he was unique." [p. 68] "Now I knew that there never was and never could have been any rivalry between us. I was not of the same quality as he." [p.70] "And I thought we were competitors! It was so ludicrous I wanted to cry." [p.79] "Friendliness, simple outgoing affection, that was all I could hear in his voice." [p.100] "Phineas was a poor deceiver, having had no practice." [p.138]

The above quotes might be highly romanticized as applied to Beebo. I stopped knowing Beebo more than fifty years ago when I was eighteen and entered the seminary. Those who knew Beebo in their later years may disagree with my description of him, using quotes from Knowles's book.

34

After a year of pinsetting at the Polish American Club, when I was 12, I was promoted to the job of racking pool. My two older brothers, Joe and Walt, got me the job. The four pocket billiard tables were located at the back of the club, beyond the bowling alleys. I worked only one day a week, Sunday from ten in the morning till midnight. I was paid three dollars for 14 hours' work. Sometimes I would get a tip for bringing drinks, but not very often. I would come home from the eight o'clock Mass, get the doughnuts, cheese cake, apple cake from Kolecki's Bakery, have breakfast and walk the ten minute walk to work. It was a clean job, except for the cigarette smoke, and it wasn't hard, but it was tiring by the end of the 14-hour day. The job was prestigious for a 13-year-old, and I felt important. I had four pool tables to take care of; I had a cash register of my own; I held $10, $25, $50, $100 bets between pool shooters; I acted as a waiter, serving hard liquor to the pool players, and I had complete control over these tables because I had the only pool rack in the house. Without me, nobody could shoot pool. I was that important.

One of the tables was of championship tournament size and three were smaller recreational tables. After each game, I racked the balls and collected the money and placed the money in a cash register in the far corner of the club. How much money I collected, depended on the game played. A game of rotation, in which you had to knock the balls in succession in any pocket, one through fifteen ball, was 25 cents; a game of 25 points, in which you knocked in any ball in a designated pocket, 50 cents; a game of 50 points, a dollar; a game of 100 points, a dollar and a half. In rotation, I placed the one ball in the beginning of the triangular rack, the two and three balls in the two back corners of the triangle and the 15 ball in the middle. Whoever knocked in the balls with the highest total of numbers on them won the game of rotation. The one with the least amount of points was the loser and usually had to pay for the game and usually for the drinks as well. In a game of points, whoever reached the designated total first won. Usually, only two players played points. They kept score by sliding beans strung on a wire above the table with their cue sticks. Sometimes the players played the game of nine-ball. I racked up only nine balls, one through nine, with the nine ball in the middle. It was a truncated form of rotation. Whoever pocketed the nine ball won the game. Sometimes they played 2, 5, 10, 15, a gambler's game. In a game of rotation, only those four balls, as well as total points, counted. Another gambler's game rarely played was called pill-ball. I had a leather pouch that contained pills with numbers 1 to 15 on them. I would roll out one pill to each player. This would determine the order in which he played. The lowest number would shoot first, etc. I would collect the pills and roll out the pills again. One to each player. This time the players would not reveal what number they got, for it was their winning number. Whoever's ball, no matter who knocks it in, is knocked in first wins the game.

Practically every Sunday, Curley, a short, red curly-haired number writer, and Jabbo, a young, smartly dressed con-artist, dominated the championship table as long as Curley's money held out. I held the bets. Each would give me twenty dollars and play 25 points. Then they would give me forty dollars and play 50 points, keeping score by moving the beads strung on a wire above the table. These games often attracted crowds because they were probably the two best players in the club. By early evening, Curley, persistent but out-classed by the younger Jabbo, would be broke and quit. And Jabbo never gave me a tip, even though I held their bets and even though I brought them drinks all afternoon.

I often had trouble serving multiple drinks. The rotation players would holler out, "Wimp, bring me a Kesslers." Another would say, "Bring me a Calverts." Another would say, "Bring me a Four Roses, a Carstairs," etc. and throw me a five or ten dollar bill. I would grab a tray from the bar and give the order to the bartender. I would try hard to remember what drink was what, but by the time I got back to the table and switched the tray around from how I got it from the bar, I invariably forgot what drink was what. When somebody asked for his Kesslers or his Calverts I would point to any drink—and they drank it and never knew the difference. So much for those connoisseurs of fine whiskeys at the Polish American Club.

After about six months, the prestige of the position of racking pool wore off. I was tired of spending my Sundays in this smoke-filled club and the pay was terrible. I could make more money setting pins, I thought. I voiced my complaint to my brother Joe and threatened to quit.

"Why don't you start knocking down, Wimp?"

"What do you mean?"

"When you collect a quarter, ring up fifteen cents on the register and pocket the dime."

I started knocking down, but my conscience bothered me. I was stealing. How could I go to Holy Communion without confessing it? How could I have true repentance or true sorrow when I knew I was going to continue to do it? I was in a dilemma. I justified my knocking down by an innate sense of what I learned much later in the seminary: the moral principle of "Occult Compensation," which put in simple terms says, "If you know you're getting ripped off, it's all right to steal to make things right because, actually, you are not stealing. You're only taking what's coming to you." I may not have known then the technical moral term involved but this was a clear case of the moral principle, Occult Compensation. Being paid $3.00 for 14 hours of work on a Sunday, was definitely not fair to me. So, I rationalized: "I really wasn't knocking down. I was just paying myself what I deserved." Instead of turning in $40 or $50 at the end of the day, I was turning in $30 or $40, and I was pocketing the rest. On Saturday afternoon I might have confessed to the priest that I swore (which I did rarely) or that I heard a swear word or that I lied or that I disobeyed my mother, but I never confessed that I stole from the Polish American Club. My conscience was clear in that regard. I was a moral theologian at an early age and didn't know it.

"This is more like it," I thought. "This job isn't so bad after all. In fact, it's a gold mine." This knocking down, or occult compensation, continued for several months, during which time I, at the age of 13, was treated like a full member of the club. I was afforded the full privileges of a member. Often I would come on a Saturday afternoon with a "guest," (Sometimes it would even be Beebo, if I were really desperate.) and bowl a few games, shoot a few games of pool, shoot some darts, some shuffle board, go to the bar and order a soda—all on the house. At 13, the Polish American Club was my Saturday afternoon hangout. I was known by everybody as Wimpy, a likeable kid, a pretty good bowler, pool shooter, dart shooter and shuffle board player for his age. Being the younger brother of Joe Crane and Tarz, two stalwarts of the club, only enhanced my reputation and prestige at the club.

Everything was going along swimmingly, until the heavy hand of justice, of the newly-elected president, who campaigned on the platform that he would root out the practice of knocking down. (It seemed everybody was knocking down: from the lofty, powerful club manager, Vince Dombrowski, down to the lowly pool table racker, me. There must have been a lot of Occult Compensations going on.) The president was an older man who spoke no English. He was squat, always dressed conservatively in a dark suit and tie and wore a fedora that he wore indoors all the time, like a Mafia figure out of the movies. Late one Sunday evening near quitting time, with my back to him working the register and in the process of knocking down, he tightly grabbed my shoulder, spun me around. and with his finger in my startled face, accused me of knocking down and fired me on the spot. He was watching me closely from the bar for the past few hours, he said. He said he caught me red handed, and he did. I was so startled I began to cry. My two brothers, Joe and Walt, appealed my case at the next club meeting, claiming that I wasn't paid enough to begin with. I had a right to knock down. In other words, they invoked the principle of Occult Compensation. But the club members didn't buy it. I guess they weren't as morally sophisticated as the Chrzanowski family.

Thus ended my rich, rewarding career at the Polish American Club. Not only was it rich, rewarding financially but socially as well. No longer was I welcomed there on Saturday afternoons to shoot pool, to bowl, to shoot darts, to play shuffle board. I never entered the club until a few years later when, now a sophomore varsity bowler at Northeast Catholic High School, I returned to bowl for the Royal Café team, of which my brother Joe was the captain. It was sort of a vindication, a sort of triumphant return.

35

As I said, Beebo seemed to have preternatural, superhuman powers. We were in awe of him; we had complete trust and confidence in him; we never saw him fail in anything he tried. I recall one Friday evening we were over Beebo's house, which consisted of the backroom of his father's bar on the corner of Edgemont and Madison Streets. Rather than go downstairs to the basement to box with boxing gloves and/or with folded up cardboard boxes to beat one another's brains out in the dark, for a diversion, Beebo suggested we take a ride in his father's car that was sitting outside the bar on Madison Street. "Are you sure it's a good idea, Beeb?" I asked. "Yeah, sure, why not?" "Do you know how to drive, Beeb?" "Yeah, I know how to drive," answered the 12-year-old Beebo, annoyed that anyone questioned his driving abilities. If he did know how to drive, he probably learned from watching his father drive, I figured.

With his father and mother busy running the bar, Beebo grabbed the keys lying on the kitchen table and the four of us, Beebo, Beerzy, Schnooky, Beebo's cousin, and me, hopped in the big black Buick sedan, just waiting to be driven. Beebo turned on the ignition; he put the car in gear and we started to move slowly, haltingly. He then jostled the gear into the next gear with a grinding noise and the car almost stalled. I began to have my doubts about Beebo's driving abilities. He brought the car to a halt when we reached Thompson Street. He made a right turn on to Thompson Street, a busy street, and made the gearshifts more smoothly this time. We drove along smoothly up Thompson Street to Venango Street where Beebo then turned right and a few blocks later made another right on to Richmond Street. We were now heading home after this ten-minute jaunt. Beebo now had his confidence behind the wheel and decided to spice things up a bit by going faster to overtake and pass the #15 trolley that was plodding along ahead of us on Richmond Street on its way to the carbarn at Allegheny Avenue.

This is when I got nervous, when all of us got nervous, except Beebo. Richmond Street was a busy, cobble-stoned street with trolley tracks running down its center. It was a dark moonless night and it was raining heavily that night. I could see from the front seat the wet shiny cobblestones and tracks glisten under our headlights, which made the driving all the more slippery and treacherous. And I wasn't sure that Beebo could see what I saw because Beebo was a small 12-year-old, smaller than I, whose feet just about touched the pedals and who could barely see above the dashboard. Beebo then gunned the Buick, trying to overtake and pass the 15 trolley, as it plodded along south on Richmond, seeking its haven at the carbarn at Allegheny Avenue. He gunned the old Buick more. We were alongside the trolley, slipping slightly on the cobble stones, alongside the wobbly trolley, with about six inches to spare on our left between us and the trolley and about six inches to spare on our right between us and the curb, the big Buick careening down Richmond Street still trying to pass the wobbly trolley for what seemed like an eternity and what seemed, at the time, at breakneck speed. But we did finally pass it, just in time for Beebo to put on the brakes and screech to a sliding halt at Allegheny Avenue when the green traffic light turned red. That was our joy ride for the night, compliments of Beebo. A joy ride I'll never forget. Beebo then slowly and carefully drove the car through heavy traffic along Allegheny Avenue back home and parked the car where he found it, returned the keys where he found them, and we went downstairs to the basement to bash each other's brains out with boxing gloves and folded cardboard boxes in the dark. Was I afraid? Naw. Excited? Yes. What was there to be afraid of? The incomparable, peerless Beebo was driving, wasn't he?

Beebo and I palled around quite a bit when we were small. I secretly admired, envied and was jealous of his remarkable athletic abilities. He also had some idiosyncrasies. I still remember he showed up around the corner with his prematurely thinning hair slicked down tight. "What are you putting on your hair, Beeb?" Beerz, with his appropriate name, although unknowing at the time, asked. "Beer. Beer's good for your hair," Beeb defensively answered. "Get the hell outta here," Beerzy replied quizzically and then smelled Beebo's hair. "Yeah, it's really beer," said Beerzy. I don't know where Beebo heard that beer was good for hair, but he didn't win any converts among us. Most of us stayed with our Vitalis, our Wildroot, our Brylcream. But Beebo stayed with his beer probably because he always had ready access to beer. He grew up in bars. His grandfather owned a bar. His father owned a bar.

Beebo's father was a handsome dapper man. He often strolled around the neighborhood, neatly dressed, sometimes carrying a cue stick in a leather case on his way to probably hustle some pool shooter at some club. His father married into the bar business. He first worked for and his family lived with his father-in-law, John Bosak, who owned Bosak's Cafe on Almond and

Allegheny. Mr. Gniewek then opened up his own small bar on the corner of Madison and Edgemont Streets, just opposite the convent-chapel of the nuns who taught at St. Adalbert's school. I understand the nuns opposed the opening of the bar because of its proximity to their chapel but were unsuccessful. And I never thought at the time, as I often looked at those stained glass windows and wondered what that chapel looked like, that someday I would be saying Mass there for the nuns when I was home for vacation after I was ordained. When Mr. Gniewek died, Beebo took over the bar.

By this time I was in the seminary. I came home one week out of the year for vacation to visit my mother. I frequently walked by Beebo's place on my way to visit my brother Joe's home on Edgemont Street and was often tempted to stop in Beebo's. What was the point? As seminarians, we took a pledge not to drink alcohol until we were ordained. I did stop in once, but Beebo was not behind the bar and I felt awkward as the entire bar turned around at this stranger's entrance.

36

When I started setting pins at the Bowlerdome during my freshman year of high school, after a year hiatus from setting pins when I, instead, racked pool at the Polish American Club, I was still pretty fast at pinsetting. I was able to compete against the other 40 or 50 pinsetters needed to set pins at the 40-lane Bowlerdome, even though I was probably the youngest and whitest of the pinsetters. Many were older Blacks, whose mere appearance frightened the hell out of me, a white boy from an all-white neighborhood on the other side of the city, with his first real contact with real Blacks.

The only contact I had with Blacks was with Brownie, a 60-year-old Negro, who sold crab cakes from a pushcart Friday nights at the corner of Richmond and Allegheny. Brownie, as far as I know, was the only Black man who lived in Port Richmond at the time. He lived somewhere in the Venango Street area. I don't know what he did the rest of the week, but every Friday during the warmer months he would push his cart down Richmond Street and park it on the corner of Allegheny Avenue. He had a small stove to keep the crab cakes warm and all the necessary condiments lined the cart. He claimed they were made from Maryland crabmeat and we believed him. Men coming from work on the 15 trolley and the 60 trolley would buy a half dozen or so for their Friday night meatless dinner. Others, like us kids, would buy one and eat it immediately as we hung out at the corner. They were big and delicious; they were a treat and they were a little too expensive for our pocketbooks: 40 cents apiece. We bought them only when we were in the chips, which was rare. Some would rather commit a mortal sin and have a cheaper hamburger or hot dog from nearby Pep's Restaurant if they were hungry on a Friday night.

Port Richmond was and still is, I believe, "Lily White." There were no Blacks living in Port Richmond with the exception of Brownie. But there was plenty of racial talk and jokes about the Blacks. I remember overhearing my older brothers talk of the incident when they and a few of their friends went by car through a Black neighborhood in central Philadelphia, giving a black crow call to the Blacks as they sped through the streets, only to have a flat tire. They dared not stop; if they did, they were dead. So they continued riding on a flat tire until they got to a white neighborhood and safety, with a shredded tire and a ruined rim.

I recall, too, coming out of a baseball game at Shibe Park at 21st Street and waiting for the 60 trolley car at Allegheny Avenue. One of the wise guys in our group made a racial slur against a passing Black. He soon came back with about a dozen of his friends, just as the 60 arrived. Thank God. We would have been dead, I think.

I recall my brothers Walt and Joe taking me to the Cambria to watch the fights. It was clear the overwhelmingly white audience preferred a black fighter opposing a white fighter and, of course the white audience would cheer for the white fighter.

When two black fighters appeared, you could hear grunts and groans from the spectators and the frequent remark: "Where are the fighters? Where are the fighters? Put on the lights! Put on the lights! We can't see the fighters!"

At the Bowlerdome I stayed pretty much to myself; I befriended a few whites in my age group but that was all. We were invited by Mrs. Walters, the owner/manager, a nice, attractive middle-aged woman, to take advantage of the "pinsetters' lounge" near the back of the alleys if we wanted to relax when not setting pins. I took her up on the invitation. I walked into a dimly lit, smoke-filled room, with a sweet-smelling aroma to the smoke. There was no ventilation in the dungeon-like room. I saw eight or ten stupefied Black men lying on several sofas and smoking what I then thought were cigarettes. I saw another five or six Blacks huddled around a round table, with a pile of money in front of them, playing cards. They all stared at me. They said nothing but their stares said, "What are you doing here, white boy? This is for us blacks only." I abruptly left without saying a word and I never entered the "pinsetters' lounge" again.

We were paid $1.25 for a league match and 15 cents plus tip for an open game at the Bowlerdome, far better wages than I received at the Polish American Club. Sometimes when there was a shortage of pinsetters for a league match, we had to jump alleys. That meant we had to set pins for two alleys by jumping over the ball return between the two alleys. It was lucrative back then in the early '40s, $2.50 for two hours' work, but it also was terribly grueling, even for a young kid of 14. And it was dangerous. After a while, especially near the end of the third game, you could easily lose track of who is bowling what on what alley. Is he shooting for a spare or did he miss the spare? Is it the tenth frame? Should you set up after the first ball after the spare? Nothing, of course, was computerized as it is today. After a while, you were so exhausted you were in a trance. Often, you would be bent over setting the pins when a ball would come rumbling down to crash into the protruding spikes.

Sometimes pins would be hurtling all over around your head, body and legs. You literally had to duck, bob and weave to avoid the pins hitting you. This happened particularly when you had a couple of pins up front and one or two in the back. Often the front pins would hit the back pins and career upward. To avoid being hit with these pins, you had two choices: using your two arms as supports, you raised your legs way up over your head and hoped the pins would hit the back of your legs; or you could run up the alley and dodge the ball. We did the latter if the bowler threw a fast ball because the front pins would carom off the back pins with a great deal of height and velocity. But, of course, you also had a split second to decide which side of the alley you were going to run up to avoid the oncoming ball.

I learned a few tricks while at the Bowlerdome on how to speed up the game. During open bowling and sometimes even during league games, to help the bowlers get more strikes, we would often, as we were raising our legs to avoid the ball and pins, kick over the eight pin into the five pin just as the ball hit the head pin.

Ed Chrzanowski

Sometimes, by mistake, we prematurely kicked the eight pin into the five pin when the ball did not hit the head pin. This created some suspicion in the minds of even the poorest or newest of bowlers. "How did I get a strike after missing the head pin altogether?" they must have thought. Another trick to get more strikes was to stack the eight and nine pins up to the next row between the four and five pins and between the five and six pins. All one had to do to get a strike, in most cases, was to hit the head pin. After about a year of setting pins at the Bowlerdome, the long 60 trolley ride was getting to me. So was my stomach. I was having stomach cramps from bending over so much. I decided to quit and join Corpo as a busboy at a downtown restaurant.

37

It seemed Corpo was my personal employment agency. He found me the job at the Bowlerdome. He then found me the job at the Bellevue Court Tavern, a small, intimate, high class restaurant on a small street behind the world-famous Bellevue Stratford Hotel, made infamous later because it was the original site of the Legionnaires' Disease. Unfortunately, a few months after I started working there as a busboy, Corpo quit because it interfered with his football practice schedule at Northeast Catholic High School, which we both attended. Corpo made the team as a starting fullback. All of the guys in Port Richmond were proud of him. One of ours made the team. We had great hopes for Corpo. But Corpo's career was short-lived. Into the fifth game of the season, Corpo was kicked in the head and suffered a concussion. It was humorous and at the same time tragic to watch Corpo, circling the field, trying to find the huddle. That marked the end of Corpo's high school football career.

The Bellevue Court Tavern was owned by an elderly, nice but nervous Mr. Greenwood. He was a Roman Catholic High School graduate, the oldest Catholic high school in the city. He and I often joked as to what school was better: Roman Catholic or Northeast Catholic. The front room consisted of a long bar and about twenty tables for drinks and tavern food. The back room was smaller, darker and consisted of eight booths against the walls and four tables in the middle of the room. If there were two busboys on duty, there would be one in each room. But if there was one, he would work in the back dinner room, which was the case most of the time I worked there. During school days I took the elevated train directly from school: from the Erie-Torresdale Station to the 13th Street Station, walk through the City Hall Concourse to Broad Street and several blocks to the Bellevue Court Tavern. I would immediately go to the basement kitchen, cut the pound blocks of butter into small rectangular chips by running a wire device through the butter, and sprinkle ice throughout the chips of butter. I would then put on my white jacket and black bow tie, go upstairs and start setting the tables in the backroom. By 5 o'clock we were ready for dinner patrons. I bussed for three elderly waiters: Max, a slight stooped man, balding hair, and glasses and with a Slavic accent. Hugo was a portly bald man, who was rumored to be pro-Nazi and who had a distinctive German accent. George was a short, quick Englishman with glasses and with thinning gray hair who was always talking about his investments and who was usually drunk by 9 o'clock.

Max had the prime station: three booths and a table closest to the service station. Depending on what kind of night he had, he would tip me between a $1.00 and $1.50. He must have been doing well because he was sending a son through college on his waiter's salary. Hugo had three booths against the far wall. He tipped me 75 cents regardless of what his night was like. He tipped me less because, as he told me almost every night, "I have only three booths." George tipped me $2.00, $3.00 depending on how soon he got drunk, and how soon I had to take over waiting on his two smaller booths and three tables at the far end of the room. And I received occasional tips from the customers. One customer must have tipped me hundreds of dollars during my tenure at the Bellevue Court Tavern. Every time he appeared at George's booth with his woman companion, I would warm three breadsticks on a hotplate, cover them with a cloth napkin, and put some extra butter on the plate. He would give me a dollar tip for this extra service every time.

Mr. Greenwood would frequently oversee the operation by standing at the bar near the food service station. From there he could watch the bar and the food operation at the same time. I recall the waiters calling out these strange sounding drinks to the bartenders: "two Martinis, a Manhattan, three Daiquiris, a Whiskey Sour, a Bloody Mary," etc. I never heard these drinks when I was racking pool and serving drinks at the Polish American Club. All I ever heard there was "four beers, a Schenley, a Calvert, a Four Roses, a Kessler," etc.

The kitchen was downstairs. Everything was transported by a dumbwaiter, which was a problem. Often orders were backed up. The waiters would call down for their food; I would call down for clean dishes and silverware. After I was there for awhile my timing with the dumbwaiter became so exquisite that I could throw down the dumbwaiter as hard as I could and just catch the brake and stop the dumbwaiter a fraction of an inch before it hit the bottom.

There was always a pot of coffee brewing in the tight service station for the waiters. Even though Mr. Greenwood lurked around the service station most evenings, keeping tabs on everything, George still managed to sip his scotch—out of his coffee cup. By 9 o'clock when Mr. Greenwood left for the day, George was in no shape to take care of his tables. I did everything but take the orders, which was just about all that George was able to do. Of course, when I did all this for George, I neglected Max and Hugo who often became upset with me to the point that Max lost his composure one evening and called me a "dumb

Polack," the first, but not the last, time I ever heard that expression.

During the summer months I worked lunches and dinners and was earning $50, $60 a week, more money than my father earned at his factory job. But the hours were long. I would leave the house at 10 o'clock in the morning and not return home until 11 o'clock at night, six days a week. I often gave my mother money when she asked. I "lent" money to my brothers, reluctantly, because I knew I would never see that money again. On Sundays, I had plenty of money to gamble with. And Mom had plenty of doilies, napkins and handkerchiefs in the house because I invariably forgot to return to the restaurant the napkins that I kept in my back pocket while bussing tables.

I enjoyed the experience and learned a great deal from it. In French class, for example, I was the only one who knew that a *filet mignon* was a steak and not a fish. I learned how to set a table, what utensils to use, how to carry six cups and saucers of coffee in one hand, and how to carry four platters, full or empty, in one hand. We were forbidden to use trays. It was considered unfashionable.

But like all good things, my time at the Bellevue Court Tavern came to an end. I was tired of the long hours, the long El ride and so before I began my senior year at Northeast Catholic I gave Mr. Greenwood my two-week notice. They all were really sorry to see me leave, especially George.

38

One Saturday afternoon I was engaged in a sport more befitting a youth my age than hanging out in a social club: weight lifting at Junior Majka's makeshift gymnasium in a one-car garage across from his home on Mercer Street. There was a heavy, hurried pounding on the door. "Wimp, are you in there? Hurry up, open up." I opened the garage door. "Get dressed. You're coming with us."

Joe and Walt, as was their wont on Saturday afternoons, were at the Polish American Association Club and after a few drinks got into an argument with Jimmy "Dickles" Boyce, a neighborhood numbers writer, the highest average bowler in the league and one of the few Irish members of the club. Dickles challenged Joe to a bowling match for money. Joe, a not so bad lefty, was no match for Dickles. Instead, Joe said he would match me against Dickles.

The club was crowded for a Saturday afternoon. The whole length of the bowling alley was lined two-deep with onlookers and bettors. I believe I was the sentimental favorite but Dickels was the clear favorite. He had a 184 average; I had a 175 average. I believe Joe and Walt bet every cent they owned on me that day. As I lined up for my first delivery, it seemed strange to see two grown men, two prominent members, two excellent bowlers, setting pins for me, where just a few short years ago I was setting pins for them.

Luckily, I was on that afternoon. The two-fingered, 16-pound house ball I used was working perfectly, hooking nicely with plenty of action, carrying the five and ten pins on light hits and kicking over the four-seven pins and six-ten pins on heavy hits. As we got into the third game of this three-game total pin match, Dickles was slightly ahead of me. The crowd got louder; I got tenser. I don't remember my exact score but it was in the 200s and I won the match by a few pins. Joe and Walt congratulated me, bought me a soda at the bar and told me to go back to my weightlifting, which I did.

Joe and Walt thought they were going to get rich by me. About a month later, they entered me into a citywide bowling tournament in downtown Philadelphia. I did well but just enough to get back their entrance fee. That was the end of that get rich quick scheme.

39

I mentioned Curly, a numbers writer; I mentioned Jimmy "Dickels" Boyce, a numbers writer. There were many numbers writers in Port Richmond. Baron was probably the best known of the small number writers because he hustled the housewives (for their numbers' business, of course). He would go house to house, street to street, collecting a five-cent bet from one, a ten-cent bet from another, and sometimes a 25-cent bet from someone who had a hot tip that day. My father, when he wasn't working days, spent hours every morning poring over the comic pages, looking for hidden numbers in the comic characters. He saw a six in Joe Palooka's ear; a zero in the button flying off Wimpy's shirt in the Popeye cartoon, etc. He bought dream books that interpreted your dreams and told you what numbers your dreams were predicting. As young as I was, I was wise enough to know this was stupid. I told my father so, not in those words, but he didn't believe me. When he found three numbers in the comics or in the dream books, he would bet them.

Numbers seemed like a constant topic of conversation in all the neighborhood. "What was the number today?" "Did you hear so-and-so hit for a quarter yesterday?" "I should have boxed my number. I would have won. I played 331 and 133 came out." Number betting was illegal, but it was blatant and open. I saw Baron taking numbers while waiting for the 60 trolley to go to court for numbers writing. Numbers writers were highly regarded by the community. They dressed nicely; they walked the streets for a few hours a day, and they all seemed to have nice homes, nice cars and plenty of money.

Much later in life, my brother Joe got involved in numbers writing. It was an easy way to make some extra money. Somebody must have squealed on him because his home was raided. Two detectives showed their badges and their search warrants. Joe wasn't home but his wife Jean, a conservative, religious, pious person, was. She casually sat in her easy chair with her feet on the footstool the whole time the two detectives searched the house, top to bottom, looking for number slips, slips of papers with the numbers and bets recorded on them. After several hours, the frustrated detectives gave up the search and left. Soon as they left, Jean got up, locked the front door to prevent them from coming back, opened the top of the footstool, grabbed the hundreds of number slips in the footstool, put them into a bag and burned them in the garbage can in the backyard. That was the end of Joe's bookmaking or numbers writing in the neighborhood. Jean was so frightened, so embarrassed that she would never endure that fright, that embarrassment again.

So Joe had to restrict his number writing to work-time only. After about 25 years of work at Kopper's Coke in Bridesburg on Richmond Street, Joe was promoted to foreman. He had access to all the workers in his department. He would go to the men, take their bets and phone the bets in during his lunch hour. Joe was doing this for several months. He was also active in the union, agitating for a new contract. One day while phoning in his bets, a detective behind him said, "You are under arrest." Joe's banker bailed him out of jail that very day, but the banker couldn't save Joe's job. He was summarily fired after 25 years—with no pension, no benefits, no insurance.

But Joe got back on his feet by buying a small, one-truck meat delivery route for $1,500 and slowly building it up until he made a comfortable living out of it, until he had a stroke and had to retire.

It was rumored in the neighborhood that the local numbers kingpin, the big banker, was Jaszko. He accumulated so much money as a numbers banker that he was able to buy the magnificent but long-abandoned bank, since Depression days, on the corner of Edgemont and Allegheny Avenues and used it as his private residence. Whenever a numbers writer got a bet for $5.00 (payoff: $2,000) or more, he would give the bet to Jaszko to bank. With odds 1,000 to 1 and the payoff 400 to 1, the odds were heavily in Jaszko's favor. He became very rich very quickly banking the higher bet numbers.

He also ran floating crap games, much like Damon Runyon's Nathan Detroit in "Guys and Dolls," in the small side streets of Port Richmond. One night, I remember coming home after playing basketball at James Martin School's gymnasium at Richmond and Ontario Streets, under the streetlight at the corner of Webb and Madison Streets, near Beebo's father's bar, was Jaszko running a crap game with about 8 or 10 players. Jaszko was the house, the banker. Everybody was betting against Jaszko. He knew each player's bet by placing the appropriate bill or bills between the fingers of his two hands. I watched a while, ran a few errands for cigarettes, made a few tips and moved on home.

In numbers playing, the first three numbers were determined by a certain digit of the amount of money bet on the first three races at a designated racetrack. That way the numbers couldn't be fixed because nobody could know how much would be bet on a race. What digit of the total bet on a race and what racetrack was being used would be revealed by a code in the

Philadelphia Daily News. My brother Joe could tell my father what the number was before the number writer told him the next day.

The real number bettors, not the housewives and men like my father, who placed ten cents on a clue from a cartoon character or a dream book, were those who played the leads, i.e., individual numbers. They would bet on one number at a time. The minimum bet was one dollar and the pay-off was 8 to 1. Not bad odds, much better than betting on all three numbers. After the first three races were finished, the bookies and bettors would meet at Richmond and Allegheny to place their bets and know within 15 minutes by telephone after the race was wagered whether they won or lost. (Whenever I had a dollar and was in the vicinity, I would place a bet on a lead, and I won several times.) And when cops not on the take were on duty, the action moved behind the billboards on Richmond and Allegheny Avenues, diagonally across from the corner where Pep's Restaurant was.

40

We kids had many a great time when Beebo's parents owned the bar, not in the bar, of course, but in the kitchen behind the bar and in the basement under the bar. We would gather on Friday nights to box in the basement. Beebo was the only one of the gang who owned two pairs of boxing gloves. Two of us would take turns squaring off against each other. But this arrangement was boring to the bystanders. So we devised a more exciting game. If there were four of us, we would each get a single glove, put out the lights and whack at one another in the dark. If there were more than four of us, we would each get a single glove and the additional kids got a folded up cardboard liquor carton to use in place of a glove, and we put out the lights and wacked at one another in total darkness. I was always at a slight advantage. I was certain to get the glove I wanted, the left-handed glove, because I was the sole southpaw in the crowd. To say the least, this was an exciting game: walking as cautiously and quietly as possible—only to have a carton or a glove, out of the dark, hit you in the face or over the head. And it could have been dangerous. One time I was pushed backward by the blow from somebody's glove. To break my fall, I put back my right gloveless hand into a box of broken liquor bottles that Mr. Gniewek threw down periodically from a trapdoor behind the bar above. (As I type this, 60 years later, I can still locate the scar on my right wrist.) Luckily, I cut my wrist between my veins and arteries there. I don't know what would have happened if I had cut a vein or artery. I wouldn't have known for several minutes that I was bleeding because of the darkness, and I don't think we knew enough to apply a tourniquet.

By this time it would be 11:00 P.M., time to go upstairs to the kitchen for some leftover fresh shrimp. Mrs. Gniewek would bring us a huge bowl of shrimp that was unsold that Friday night. We ate so much shrimp every Friday night that after a while I grew to dislike shrimp. I couldn't eat a shrimp again until well into the priesthood.

41

Numbers writing was Beebo's ruination. His popular tavern was raided a number of times, closed down and reopened. He was arrested for paying off the cops. But Beebo, the story goes, got a little avaricious, took too big a chance. Instead of passing off the bigger bets to the big bankers like Jaszko who could absorb big losses, he began to back them himself until one day somebody placed a $50 bet on a number and the number came out, which cost Beebo $20,000. That was the end of Beebo's Tavern; he shut the doors for good, and to a great extent, it was the end of Beebo. He couldn't survive without that tavern; he had no other means of income.

Ed Chrzanowski

Port Richmond's 'Bootin' Bartender'

By HUGH BROWN

THE PICTURE showed ten dazzling co-eds lining up in glamor formation before a flossy sorority house and casting toothy, covetous smiles at the Big Man of the Campus, a handsome youth who had carried a football farther than any other collegian in the nation.

The recipient of this platoon adoration was fullback Bill MacPhail, the battering bucko of the University of Oklahoma, who can scarcely evade somebody's All-American. MacPhail is an overpowering six feet, four inches in height and 230 pounds in heft, or a size that enhances anyone's progress, either with foot...

Len 'Beebo' Gniewek
A Big Little Man

For a perverse reason, the picture was reminiscent of another one, far removed, that hangs in a candy store in the northeast section of this sprawling city. The picture in the candy store was taken on a field cluttered with crab grass and shows the Venango Bears' amateur football team lined up in sequence around the big, small man of Port Richmond's sandlots.

The big, small man of the sandlots is the Bootin' Bartender, Len (Beebo) Gniewek, a lantern-jawed stripling who is only five feet eight inches in height and 150 pounds in heft, or of a size that would not excite a high school coach, far less a co-ed. But a couple of weeks ago, Beebo booted a 51-yard field goal, or only two yards short of the record in the National Professional Football League. And Beebo is merely a Mastbaum Vocational alumnus and a non-fraternity man.

Rival Nixes Penalty That Would Have Voided Kick

AFTER left halfback Gniewek (pronounced Gniewek) kicked the pigskin such a monstrous distance, the referee made motions as if to step off a penalty and thus nullify the feat. The manager of the opposing Holy Child team sprang from the bench, glowered at the official and yelled:

"Get away from there. I've never seen anything like it before and I'm not going to let you spoil it."

During the same afternoon, the Bootin' Bartender reeled off runs of 80, 55, and 60 yards, kicked all the extra points, and otherwise made himself useful. He explained that he has kicked only two field goals this season—the other was a 35 yarder—because his self-educated toe hasn't been needed in the Bears' accumulation of 166 points for themselves and only six for their opponents.

Beebo Gniewek has been playing sandlot football seven years, during which time he has read about every sports book ever published and remembered most of their contents. Besides, kicking, running, passing and coaching, he has accumulated considerable knowledge of the T formation, the single and double wings, flankers, spinners, loops and slants.

The Bears' left halfback learned how to kick a football by diligent practice under the eye of an older brother who lectured him on the wisdom of "keeping your head down when you bring your toe up." Beebo bought a pair of kicking shoes this season that cost $28. He only uses the right shoe and wouldn't mind locating a left-footed kicker who would give him $14 for the boot he doesn't use.

This summer, the pride of the Venango Bears was taken to the Eagles' training camp at Hershey under the wing of Mike Jarmoluk, the Birds' 230-pound tackle who is also a Beebo admirer. The Eagles' coaches took a look at the scant Gniewek frame and then let him get lost in a large mound of discarded campus heroes.

The 19-year-old Beebo in his prime. 1948.

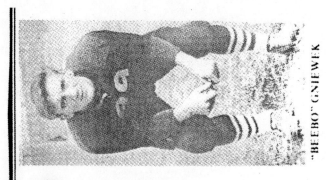

"BEEBO" GNIEWEK

The Venango Bears

THE LEGENDS OF THE BEARS

For over 50 years the stories of the Venango Bears and their players have been told and retold, until it's hard to separate truth from myth. The tales of Monk Dietz, Danny Lano, Mickey McFadden, Les Dunn and Jack Svitak have reached a stage where their names are mentioned only with great respect by the old Bears. The young Bears speak of them as if they were national heroes.

One name seems to dominate any conversation concerning the Bears. The name Len Gniewek might not cause a ripple, but just drop the name "Beebo," and you will hear stories and stories...for a thousand years or a thousand beers, whichever you prefer.

The first time the Bears saw Beeb, he was a skinny kid that had never played organized football, but in seven seasons he became THE Greatest Legend in Venango Bear history. The term "He's a natural" has for years been used to describe great athletes, but never was it ever truer than in the case of Beebo Gniewek, for here was a REAL "Natural."

Beebo, a legend in his own time.

Ed Chrzanowski

He was well known as a great athlete throughout Port Richmond for many years, until he was well into his forties. His reputation extended to Bridesburg, another Polish enclave immediately north of Port Richmond, and to Fishtown, a predominantly Irish neighborhood with St. Anne's Parish on Lehigh Avenue at its center, immediately south of Port Richmond. With Beebo at shortstop and batting fourth, until his early 50s, Beebo's Tavern teams were always competitive. His teams and opponents would come back to his place and drink well into the morning. He still was a remarkable athlete at that age.

Not only was he a remarkable sandlot athlete in all sports, he played high school football briefly at Northeast Catholic, and after he was expelled from there, at several public high schools. He was relatively small in stature, about 5'8", about 150 pounds. He was a triple threat back. He could run, pass, and punt. He kicked extra points and 40-yard field goals by dropkicking the ball, by kicking the ball as it touched the ground after he dropped it. He did not have blazing speed but he was shifty and quick. He could change directions on a dime, and he could have made a name for himself beyond the neighborhood, many say, if he were only more disciplined in his youth. He never cracked a book in high school; he frequently skipped school, skipped practices and he was eventually dropped from every high school team he briefly played for. He bounced from school to school with poor grades until it was too late for him to go to college. But his reputation as a sandlot football player, after high school, caught the attention of the Philadelphia Eagles. They invited him to their training camp, at nearby Hershey, for a tryout as a punt and kickoff return specialist. Beebo was cut on the last day of tryouts.

The last time I saw Beebo was in the vestibule of St. Adalbert's Church. After I left the priesthood. I went to Sunday Mass and who was one of the ushers, one of the collectors? Surprisingly, Beebo. I say surprisingly because Beebo was not very religious as a kid as far as I knew, although, naturally, he was a good kid, I thought. We reminisced a bit and I gave him a warning in the form of a true story my father told years ago. This certain usher/collector, rain or shine, always carried an umbrella to Sunday Mass. One rainy Sunday morning he forgot himself and opened the umbrella when he got out into the rain. Then pennies, dimes, quarters, half dollars of the Sunday collection rained down on his fedora. According to my father, the mortified man never went back to St. Adalbert's Church.

Still living in the same building that housed the bar, Beebo died of cancer, leaving a widow and two grown sons. I understand, from his older brother, Gene, a prominent Port Richmond funeral director, the funeral was well attended, worthy of a celebrity, of a legend. Encomiums, eulogies, tributes were written up in the local press about Beebo. All kinds of sports memorabilia were buried with him, according to his brother, Gene, who should have known since he was the funeral director. Here are some of the obits and testimonials written by local sportswriters when Beebo died in 1988 at the age of 59:

Hugh Brown, sportswriter for *The Evening Bulletin*, wrote: "The big, small man of the sandlots is the Bootin' Bartender. Len (Beebo) Gniewek, a lantern-jawed stripling who is only five feet eight inches in height and 150 pounds in heft. A couple of weeks ago, Beebo booted a 51-yard field goal, or only two yards short of the record in the National Professional Football League....During the same afternoon, the Bootin' Bartender reeled off runs of 80, 55, and 60 yards, kicked all the extra points, and otherwise made himself useful....The [Venango] Bears' left halfback learned how to kick a football by diligent practice under the eye of an older brother who lectured him on the wisdom of "keeping your head down when you bring your toe up."

Jim Nicholson of the Philadelphia *Daily News* wrote: "Beebo was a left halfback who also could rifle a ball 60 yards on a jump pass.... He played halfback on defense and was known as a hard tackler. He once got knocked out twice in one game. Home games in which Beebo was playing could draw 2,000 spectators….He also had other skills. He was a pool shark who loved to hustle nine-ball….He was known equally as a soft touch and tough street fighter….He could collect bets one day and take up the collection in church the next."

Shortly after his death, several stories, true or apocryphal, as happens to almost all legends, began to surface. Beebo loved to gamble. He would bet on almost anything and most of the time he would win. One story, recounted by his older brother Gene, a not exactly reliable source, I admit, but who vouches for its authenticity is that before a Richmond Redskins football game at the homefield at Richmond and Allegheny Avenues, Beebo sauntered over to the sidelines to Jaszko, the big numbers banker, and said, "I'll betcha 50 bucks I score the first time I touch the football." "You're on," replied the excited Jaszko, thinking he had a sucker bet. The opposing team kicked off. The ball sailed into Beebo's arms on the five-yard line and I was witness to the following, for I blocked for Beebo on this particular play. He went straight up the middle of the field for about 20 yards, evading a few would-be tacklers, and then sharply turned to the left sideline, right by the awe-stricken Jaszko, standing on the opponent's 20 yard line, and went all the way, untouched, into the end zone for a touchdown.

He had his faults as we all do. (Being a braggadocio was not the least of his faults.) But as far as I am concerned, there will never be another Beebo. He truly was a legend in his own time. (Some detractors would say "he was a legend in his own mind." Maybe this memoir may shed some light on the controversy.)

42

As I said earlier, it was a rich, rewarding experience to work and hang out at the Polish American Club. I learned to bowl, to shoot pool; to shoot darts, to shuffle discs. Whenever there was a table open at the Polish American Club, I would pick up a cue stick and shoot some pool; and whenever I wasn't too busy racking up pool, I would mosey over to the nearby dart board and shoot some darts, or go over to the shuffle board and shuffle some discs. I became very proficient at these "indoor sports."

The experience stood me in good stead later in life when I shot pool and shuffle board at the subterranean Lithuanian Club at Tilton and Allegheny and shot darts at Gutowicz's Bar at the corner of Salmon and Allegheny across from Harry's Ice Cream Parlor. I made a lot of money and drank a lot of beer at those two establishments because of my proficiency at those healthy, wholesome indoor sports.

Most of us were under age, 16, 17, to shoot darts and drink beer, but nobody at Gutowicz's Bar seemed to care. We shot darts for money and for beers almost every night for four or five hours and I would stagger home almost every night. After a few weeks of this behavior, the thought occurred to me: "Maybe I'm becoming an alcoholic at the age of 16." And this is when I began to think seriously of the priesthood, not that alcohol and priesthood necessarily go together. I just didn't want to spend the rest of my life hanging out in bars and clubs and getting drunk, hanging out on street corners, discussing the number that came out that day, discussing ball scores, discussing conditions at work, discussing which girls were easy and which weren't, discussing who beat up whom, whistling at girls as they passed by, trying to make out with them in Harry's Ice Cream Parlor, etc. I knew there was a bigger and better world out there than Port Richmond. I didn't want to be stuck in Port Richmond in some factory job for the rest of my life. There was the wider world of travel, of music, of theater, of literature. I saw the priesthood, maybe subconsciously, as an outlet, maybe my only outlet, to that world.

Perhaps I'm being too hard on myself. It's difficult to re-create how I thought back then when I was 17, an immature 17, over 50 years ago. How pure could a 17-year-old's motives be back then? How pure are anybody's motives, even a mature adult's? All religion then, particularly the Roman Catholic Church, I think, was immature, much of it based on superstition and ritual.

Actually, I thought of the priesthood since the eighth-grade when Sr. Fides inculcated the idea. She would drop subtle hints, a suggestion, now and again. I remember attending a religious function in the church and as she passed me by in procession she whispered to me, "*Szlicznie.*" (Excellent). But she was transferred after my eighth grade and I forgot about the priesthood until about my junior year in high school, about when I was hanging out in bars, clubs, and street corners.

I did have some spiritual motivation to enter the priesthood. I wanted to save my soul and Sr. Fides told me the way to ensure saving your soul was to save somebody else's soul and the surest way to do that was to become a priest whose vocation it was to save souls. (Perhaps a spiritual motive but still not a very unselfish one.) And I could add another not so pure motive to pursue the priesthood. I wouldn't mind the adulation the priest receives from the people. During Sunday Mass I could easily picture myself up there at the altar saying Mass, or at the pulpit preaching to the people, and I liked that picture.

During high school, I was taught by an order of priests, the Oblates of St. Francis de Sales. They seemed like regular guys who enjoyed what they were doing. I became friendly with one of them, Fr. George Godley, who was the moderator of the bowling team. One day during my senior year, on the El to a bowling match in Jimmy Dykes Bowling Alleys in center-city, I told him of my childhood aspirations. I remember telling him that I didn't think I was worthy enough to be a priest, and I meant it. I had such esteem and respect for the priesthood. He said, "Who is worthy?

Nobody is worthy to be a priest." After some soul-searching and after I found my closest friend in high school, John Murphy, was going to the Oblate seminary, I made up my mind to join the Oblates of St. Francis de Sales.

I told my father of my intentions. Surprisingly, he tried to talk me into becoming a parish priest, a diocesan priest, a secular priest. Pop knew more about the priesthood than I thought, maybe more than I did. He knew there was a vast difference between a religious order priest and a diocesan priest. If I joined the Oblates, I would take on the Vow of Poverty. If I became a diocesan priest, I would not. As a diocesan priest, I could own my own car; I could have my own bank account, and I would be most likely stationed near home somewhere in or around Philadelphia. As a religious order priest with the Vow of Poverty, I could not possess anything of my own. And with the Vow of Obedience I had to go wherever my superiors sent me. With the Oblates, I would very likely teach high school anywhere in the country or go to the missions in South

Africa or South America. The diocesan priesthood seemed more appealing to my father than the religious order priesthood. He took me to the parish rectory and hoped the diocesan priest would dissuade me from joining the Oblates. He did not. After we left the rectory, I told my father: "If I can't be an Oblate priest, I will not be a priest." He gave up trying to change my mind.

43

For a change from Gutowicz's Bar where we could shoot only darts for money and beers, we went to the underground Lithuanian Club to shoot pool or play the shuffleboard. We rang the bell and hoped that Tony the Doorman, with a fedora jauntily set on his head, was on duty because he would always let us in without question (I don't think he was able to speak or understand English.) even though we weren't members and even though all of us were way under age. But he probably figured we brought new life to an already moribund club. (It no longer exists.) We descended the five or six steps to a spacious, low- ceilinged, dimly lit, musty room. The pool table was almost always unoccupied and unattended, which meant we could play for nothing. There were two shuffle boards that were sometimes occupied and about six card tables with one or two occupied by elderly pinochle players and a bar in the back room to the left that was almost always empty.

Once in a while, if all we had was a dime each to our name, Beerzy, a good shuffle-board player and I, an excellent player, would challenge the winners of the shuffle board to play for beers. Once we got on the shuffleboard, we stayed there for hours, game after game, frustrating challengers until closing time, or until we were so drunk that we finally lost a game and had to buy our two victors two ten-cent draft beers. What made me a particularly proficient shuffleboard player was that I was equally good with either hand. If my opponent blocked the right side of the board, I would get by the blockade from the left side.

I became ambidextrous when I was very young. I was naturally left-handed but my older brothers taught me to be right-handed, thinking it would be to my advantage later, by doing everything right-handed, and I think they were right. When they threw a ball to me, they insisted I throw it back right-handed when my natural instinct was to throw it back left-handed. When I batted, I had to bat right-handed. It worked. Today, I do most things right-handed but I do some things left-handed.

In fact, even later, my proficiency at pool came in handy my first year in the seminary. On Wednesday afternoon, we seminarians were all given ten cents to buy an ice cream bar in town down the road about a mile. The town was Childs, Maryland, about three miles from Elkton, at the time the marriage capital of the world because Elkton did not require a marriage blood test and had no waiting period. Childs consisted of a general store, a post office, and a gas station. It was a joke to us from the big city of Philadelphia. Before we embarked on our trip to Childs to spend our fortune of ten cents, I would engage a few of the novices (They were actual novices in the novitiate or seminary sense and certainly novices at shooting pool.) in a game of pool at the community pool table and take away their dimes. After a few weeks of this nefarious practice, one of my victims complained to the Novice Master, who then laid down a strict edict: "There is to be no gambling in the pool room!" That was the end of a good thing. I must add that I did share my winnings with some of my buddy novices and the pool hustling did begin to bother my conscience.

Occasionally, we hopped the 60 trolley to K&A, walked a few stores past the Iris Theatre on the west side of Kensington Avenue and walked up a long, narrow stairway to a real poolroom: the K & A Pool Emporium. It must have housed twenty to thirty pool tables of different sizes. A few tables did not even have pockets. Strange, I thought at the time. The room was always dark, even during the day because the El line right outside the windows obstructed the daylight. Only the lights with green shades above the tables cast any light in the place. Dozens and dozens of pool cue sticks lined the walls. High bar chairs for players and spectators were also situated along the walls. We were always intimidated when we entered the place. First of all, we were too young. We shouldn't have been allowed in the place in the first place, but the owners, an elderly, cigar-chomping man and his wife, a young, beautiful blond, young enough to be his daughter, didn't seem to mind, as long as we didn't watch all day but shot some pool once in a while. Here you paid by the hour, $1.50 an hour, much more expensive than .25 cents for a game of rotation at the Polish American Club where I knocked down nickels and dimes and more than the Lithuanian Club where we played for free most of the time.

We really did come to watch. Here is where the pool sharks, the hustlers hung out. Here is where the stakes and drama were high. Here is where somebody could run 40 balls or more, where they knew how to play position pool. Here is where all kinds of gambling took place: numbers writing, sports betting, track betting. And the atmosphere, surprisingly, was not that unsavory. The clientele was nice; the owners were nice, friendly people as long as you had some money to spend and you didn't cause any trouble.

44

One of the most pleasant memories of my childhood experience occurred on Allegheny Avenue on Holy Thursday evening. A constant stream of people, many dressed in their Sunday finery and already wearing their Easter smiles, would stroll leisurely by as we sat on Furtek's step watching. They were on their way to visit the three churches along Allegheny Avenue just a few blocks apart and to pray for the indulgence to be gained when one visited three Altars of Repose, where the Blessed Sacrament reposed that day until tomorrow, Good Friday. If the weather was nice and it usually was, the more pious would visit a fourth and fifth church: the small wooden St.George's Church, the Lithuanian church about 5 blocks north of Allegheny Avenue on Edgemont Street, and Mother of Divine Grace Church, the Italian Church, about five blocks south on Thompson Street. Although not dressed in our Sunday best, we kids would also visit the three or five churches and then debate and argue afterwards as to which altar was most beautifully decorated. Invariably, the consensus was that the altar at St. Adalbert's Church, the Polish church, was most beautiful. And it really was because the Polish nuns who did the decorating took a special pride and made a special effort in their decorating, even though it was only for one day, which I privately thought was a waste. The fact that most of the kids engaged in the debate were of Polish extraction might have swayed our opinion a bit.

My father as a young man.

Another moving religious ceremony involving Allegheny Avenue took place on the Feast of Corpus

Christi. After the noon Sunday Solemn High Mass (with at least three priests on the altar, incense burning, choir singing, bells ringing), the entire congregation would leave the church from the main entrance on Allegheny Avenue. Passersby and people from their homes joined the throng. Escorted by other priests and dozens of altar boys, some carrying candles, others ringing bells, others swinging incensors that gave off a fragrant smoke even in the open air, the main celebrant carried an elaborately designed gold monstrance that contained and displayed the Sacred Host, the Body of Christ, the Corpus Christi. The procession winded itself around to Thompson Street, a busy street ordinarily, but on this day the traffic was diverted and it was here that I saw my father kneeling. I must have been 9 or 10. I knelt next to him. He tousled my hair and smiled affectionately, and I accompanied him throughout the hour-long procession around the entire block. I was so proud and happy as we both knelt side by side when the celebrant blessed us with the monstrance containing the Sacred Host. We proceeded around to Madison Street and another altar. Then we walked past Gniewek's Bar and then on to Edgemont Street to the entrance to the convent where another altar was set up. Finally, we arrived back at the front of the church on Allegheny Avenue, where the final benediction with the Sacred Host took place. The procession was over; people scattered in all directions. My father patted me on the head and sent me back home as he went to Big Ben's Social Club up Thompson Street for the day to play some pinochle and probably get drunk. It was the first and only time my father, not a particularly religious man, and I worshipped together.

In the summer evenings, we kids would sit on Furtek's front steps on Allegheny Avenue and watch the people, the world—our small, confined world—go by. Almost every evening around 8:30 we would see Rudy Niemiec, a blond, good-looking fellow with a chunky muscular build, approach, and we would begin to laugh quietly. Rudy had the reputation of being a street fighter, a brawler, who once had a promising career as a prizefighter until the bottle got the best of him. We laughed quietly, for fear he would hear us and become a raging bull; he would get mad at us and come after us. He was known to do that. We laughed because Rudy was walking backwards. It seemed that when Rudy had one too many drinks he was unable to walk forward without falling on his face, but he had no problem walking backwards.

During summer evenings, many of the residents of Allegheny Avenue sat on folding chairs in front of their residences or businesses and watched a constant flow of humanity stroll by, and cars ride by, and the 60 trolley car clang by. They could also look across the avenue and see what was happening on the other side, who strolled there, who entered what doctor's office, who entered what bar and in what condition he left it. They must have watched me a number of times on a late Saturday afternoon, as I helped my drunken father home from the Royal Café. I dreaded when my mother would tell me to go fetch Pop from the Royal. But I did it, I guess, out of filial loyalty. With his right arm draped around my neck and holding on to it with my right hand, and with my left arm firmly around his waist, as if he were a wounded comrade, I would dodge cars and trolleys, to bring my father home to a cold dinner and to a verbal lacing from my mother. I was deeply, deeply embarrassed every time I carried my father home, but I did it. In fact, afterward, I felt proud of myself. In fact, at the time he wasn't even heavy; he was my father.

45

During the week when he was working the day shift, my father led a Spartan existence. He had his daily bottle of beer before dinner and after dinner he would nap on the sofa in the living room until it was time to go to bed. There wasn't much jollity in our home. Rarely did my parents speak to each other, except when necessary and always seriously. That made it all the more exceptional when on occasion while in bed in the back bedroom I would hear my mother giggle when my mother and father were in bed in the front bedroom. I never could understand her unusual behavior. "Why does Mom giggle only in bed?" I asked myself.

My wife Shirley honoring the dead with two of my first cousins in Karwowa, Poland, where my father was born. All Saints Day, 1999.

My cousin Jerry with his son, daughter-in-law and grandchildren in Jedwabne, near Karwowa, Poland.

The only time my father exhibited any conviviality at home was when he coerced my three older brothers to stay home in the evening to play pinochle. Pop loved his pinochle. At first, my brothers didn't mind playing pinochle, but later as they got older they did. As a child I thought it was nice to see my three older brothers and father playing pinochle together. They never did anything as a family. I enjoyed standing by my father counting his counters— aces, kings and tens. I think that's how I first learned to count. After he died, the four of us brothers kept up that tradition. Whenever we could, especially when I came home for vacation from the seminary and later the priesthood, we would get together, buy some beer and snacks and play pinochle long into the night for a buck a game and a quarter for sets.

I remember, too, often helping my father roll his own cigarettes. He would purchase a can of Bugle tobacco that came with cigarette paper and the cigarette-rolling machine. Pop would pour a little tobacco, enough for one cigarette, into the trough of the small leather belt of the machine, slide the paper under the tobacco, and roll the completed cigarette out of the machine. He would then enclose both ends by moistening them with his mouth and pinching them together. It certainly didn't look like a professional cigarette and probably didn't taste as good but it probably was a lot cheaper.

During the week Pop led a Spartan existence, as I said, but on Saturdays and Sundays he made up for it. On Saturdays, at the Royal Café, he would drink boilermakers, a shot of whiskey with a beer chaser, all afternoon, until he couldn't walk home, and I had to carry him home. On Sundays, after the 10:30 Mass, he would go to Big Ben's Social Club (translation of *Boleslaw Wielki*i, a Polish hero), on Thompson Street between Allegheny Avenue and Clementine Street, to play pinochle and drink. Sometimes he would get so absorbed in his pinochle game that he didn't drink so much and sometimes came home somewhat sober for Sunday dinner, but that was the exception. Only social clubs with a paid membership were allowed to serve liquor on Sundays in Philadelphia at the time and there were many social clubs in Port Richmond, practically one on every other street.

I knew when Pop came home really intoxicated. That's the only time Mom had nerve to stand up to him. Mom would raise her voice to him and Pop, losing the argument, as a last resort would retaliate by using the heavily accented f... word repeatedly. It pained me and frightened me to hear my father use the f...word at my mother. I recall one time when I was 8 or 9, running out of the kitchen and cowering in the corner of the living room, screaming through tears, "Stop it! Stop it! I can't take it anymore." Pop, as drunk as he was, stopped and never again used the f... word in our presence.

Pop went to the 10:30 Sunday Mass. Mom went to the noon Solemn High Mass. I went to the eight o'clock children's Mass and my three brothers went to the nine o'clock English Mass, if they didn't instead go to the Polish American Social Club on Richmond and

Allegheny Avenues. One Sunday morning I saw my father, late for Mass, looking for his overcoat. It was upstairs. Instead of running upstairs for his coat, he put on my brother Walt's overcoat. They were about equal size. As he was going out the door, he took his rosary from a bureau drawer and put it in the pocket of the coat. Pop came home straight from Mass that day, without going to Big Ben's, which was highly unusual, and confronted Walt and tongue-lashed him (He was too big to beat or he would have beaten him.) for causing him a great embarrassment. It seems that my father because he was late had to stand in the aisle of the crowded church. He then pulled his rosary out of Walt's coat pocket and with the rosary out flew a box of prophylactics that made a loud enough slapping sound against the linoleum floor to catch everybody's attention as it hit the floor. My father, thoroughly humiliated, bent over and picked up the prophylactics as nearby worshippers gave him a look of disdain that I'll bet the woman caught in adultery in the gospels never got.

My father was a raconteur. He enjoyed telling stories when company was visiting and his adult audience seemed to enjoy listening to his stories. I found them boring and thought they would never end probably because I was too young to really understand them. I remember a key word that appeared often in his story-telling, especially in his work-related stories, "voder." "Who is this "voder?" What is this "voder?' I asked myself repeatedly for years until I finally figured it out. What an epiphany! What a revelation! I would have understood many of his stories if I had known the meaning of this all-important word, "voder." Quoting others, Pop was attempting to pronounce his name Walter in English. In Polish the "w" is pronounced as a "v."

Pop was a good-looking man, especially after he had his false teeth put in. He was about 6 feet tall with a slightly paunchy stomach, a swarthy complexion and a full head of auburn hair with not a tinge of gray hair in it. He had a pleasant disposition when sober, and lest I give the wrong impression, was most of the time.

With company, he was affable, well liked, respected; he seemed to dominate most conversations. He was a good provider. I don't remember his ever taking off from work, no matter his condition on Sunday.

He must have been an excellent provider. Before my birth in 1929, through the throes of the Depression, he brought up three boys. He bought a home; he gutted it; he renovated it; he enlarged the kitchen and added a bedroom and a bathroom above the kitchen, and he took the entire family to Poland for six months where he spent money very freely, as I was told by my cousins on a recent visit to Poland. All on a laborer's salary and moonshining, a word never uttered by my parents or its Polish equivalent, *przemytnik*. I don't remember anything about the moonshining, except discarded pipes and tanks in the corner of the basement after the repeal of Prohibition in 1933 and what Joe told me many years afterwards. It was all hush hush, nothing to be proud of because it was illegal, but, apparently, nearly everybody was doing it. According to Joe, Pop had the reputation of making the best vodka in the neighborhood.

When Pop and his older sister Felicia came to this country in 1913, they left behind in Poland parents, an older brother and two younger brothers. My grandfather's first wife died while giving birth to her only child, a son, Valentine. My grandfather then remarried and had six children. Valentine came to America, settled in Wallingford, Connecticut, where he had a prosperous corner grocery store. He helped bring Felicia to the United States, his younger half-sister and Pop, his younger half-brother, who both settled in Philadelphia, just a few blocks from each other. Felicia married and raised seven children in a home near the park on Madison Street. My Aunt Felicia often visited her younger brother and my mother on her way home from her daily Mass attendance and both families visited each other especially at holiday time. Pop's older brother, Stanley, remained in Poland because it was a tradition that the oldest boy was to take over the farm from the father, which is what happened in our recent visit to Poland. Stanley's oldest son, Andrew, my first cousin and a few years younger than I, a widower with five children, now presides over the homestead where my father was born and reared, in a tiny hamlet of Karwowa, near the city of Jedwabne, Poland. According to documents that have come recently into my possesion, thanks to Fred Cimino, a retired school teacher and unofficial archeologist and archivist of Port Richmond, my father became a naturalized American citizen June 9, 1926. Two of his neighbors, a Stanley Stankowicz, listed as a City Hall Clerk and unknown to me, and Stanley Majka, a neighbor down the street and an occasional visitor to our house, stood as witnesses for Pop when he petitioned for naturalization.

My father respected his older sister, Felicia, almost feared her, I believe, and was always subdued in her presence. My mother secretly disliked her, which she confided to me later in life when I was a priest, ever since she told my father, "You could have done much better in selecting a wife."

Ed Chrzanowski

46

My mother was short and became plump as she got older. She was a good housewife and a good mother. She was even-tempered and pleasant, except when my father came home drunk. She had a pretty face. Her hair, like my father's, was auburn with no trace of gray.

I still felt sorry that she had no feminine companionship in the house. I remember a simple discovery, an awareness that had a chilling effect on me. After my father died, as a young seminarian home on vacation, I decided to paint my mother's bathroom. While cleaning the bathroom thoroughly in preparation to painting, I found stuffed behind the cat's paw of the bathtub against the wall, a dried, caked bloodied rag that must have been there for years. I paused and thought. Without our modern products, I suppose, how often had she to dispose of these things, privately, secretly, fearing to be discovered in the process?

260

I didn't know anything of my mother's lineage in Poland when my wife and I went to Poland two years ago. I have recently learned, again from Fred Cimino, that she arrived in this country June 9, 1914, two months before the outbreak of World War I. I did know she had an older brother, Alex, who preceded her to this country and helped bring her here. He was a tall, mustached, severe man who spoke little, smoked a pipe, and drank no liquor. I recall as a very young boy spending several weeks of several summers on his farm outside of Philadelphia. I earned my keep. I spent whole days as a 6 or 7 year old, picking potatoes, carrots, beets in his fields. He had three sons and three daughters, all older than I. I don't remember the exact sleeping arrangements for all his children. All I know is that I found it strange even at that early age, to sleep between two of his daughters who must have been five or six years older than I. When all his children were grown, he sold his farm and moved into the city near my mother, who by that time was widowed. He was a big help as Mom's handy man around the house.

I remember visiting the Blusiewicz family in the country. Mr. Blusiewicz was a big man, with a red face and a booming voice and hearty laugh. The Mrs. was a roly-poly kind of woman with a gentle, sweet voice. They had two sons about my brother Joe's age. I enjoyed visiting their large well-kept farm because of the animals and because they always made homemade ice cream when we visited. They later sold the farm and bought a huge country inn nearer Philadelphia in Newportville. I believe it is still there. I remember visiting them on Friday nights when beer flowed freely and live Polish music wafted over the creek across the road, late into the night.

We also visited on Sunday afternoon the widow Pilsudska and her pig farm. I hated visiting her farm because of the stench, because of the flies all over the food, and because her farmhouse was not clean. I had a hard time eating the sumptuous meal she put out for us. I remember every adult went out into the fields to pick wild mushrooms. (Still a common practice in Poland.) They ate them for supper and my entire family, except me, on the drive home had to pull over the side of the road and retched their insides out.

47

The people who lived on Allegheny Avenue had a wonderful vista, compared to my mother's, who couldn't even afford a folding chair and who sat on a pillow on her small, white marble step to look at Furtek's garages about twenty feet in front of her and who said hello to an occasional passerby. She would also look, at a distance, to the right, at the passersby on Allegheny Avenue. I remember sitting there with my mother many an evening, out of compassion, just to keep her company. It wasn't exciting sitting on our front step, saying hello to an occasional passerby, but it beat sitting indoors in a stuffy home during the sweltering summer months.

Most of the people who lived on Allegheny Avenue had a business. They had to have a good income to maintain their homes. They were three-storied, high-ceilinged structures, and they were about three times the length of the row houses around the corner on Mercer Street where we lived.

Joe, or Googoo, as he was known throughout the neighborhood (and beyond, I think), was probably the most fascinating character in the entire neighborhood. He lived on Allegheny Avenue where his father operated a delicatessen. When we were six, seven, eight years old, we would prevail upon Googoo to tell us stories. On cold, wintry nights, about six or seven of us would huddle around him in the doorway of Furtek's Dry Goods Store on the corner of Mercer Street and Allegheny Avenue. He would then, for what seemed like hours, spin tales about his leading character, Left-to-Right-to-the-Boom, a superman type of hero who had the magical power of elongating his left and right arms to defeat the enemies of society, and of Leppe, the hideous, ghoul-like character, who scared the wits out of us.

Googoo was handsome, muscular—about six feet tall, 180 pounds, with long blond hair, sleepy, sexy bedroom eyes. He reminded me of Sterling Hayden or Guy Madison, popular movie actors at the time, or maybe a later James Dean. He was not very bright academically but he was street smart. During the summer, he always sported a deep bronze tan that he got at the shore at Wildwood, New Jersey, a popular summer resort, about 90 miles southeast of Philadelphia. He and Jimmy DiPersio lived there all summer. They supported themselves by staging wrestling matches, much after the manner of modern-day TV wrestling matches, on the beach off the boardwalk and relied on tips from passersby. (This took place in the early '40s when staged wrestling matches were still in their infancy.) They would spend the rest of the day working on their tan and prowling after girls at the nightspots after dark. They would sleep under the boardwalk until the police would awaken them and tell them to move on. If they ever got into a pinch with money, they could always hitch a ride back to Philly to show off their tan to their envious buddies, to sell a pint of their blood for $15.00 at the local Red Cross, to mooch off their family and friends, and then head back to the shore.

I don't know if Googoo ever went to school; I don't know if he ever worked. He survived by mooching (He was always broke it seems.), by his wits, and, occasionally, by pulling a dirty trick. Once, on a slow Saturday afternoon, he challenged me to a game of pool at the Polish American Club. "I'll shoot you a game of 25 points for a buck, Wimp." But I was wise to him. I knew he probably didn't have any money on him and even if he did, he wouldn't have paid me if he lost. I accepted the challenge—on my terms. "I'll shoot you a game of 50 points for a quarter." He left in disgust, muttering to himself, "How the hell is anybody to make any money, shooting 50 points for a quarter?"

I recall one Sunday morning after the 10:30 Mass, as was our custom, we started a card game right in the middle of Mercer Street just off Allegheny Avenue. There were about ten of us playing, grown ups and kids alike. (Kids were welcome to play as long as they had money to ante up.) We all anted up a quarter. The dealer bent over and dealt us all three cards, making a full circle three times to do so. It was a form of Three Card Monte but we called it Three Card Ante. The best possible hand would be three aces, a rarity. A very good hand would be a pair of aces. Any pair would be considered a betting hand, unless a lot of guys were still in the game. Sometimes one could steal the pot with ace high, another rarity.

The action began to the left of the dealer. The player could fold or play. If he plays, he must put in 50 cents. In this particular hand, the player next to the dealer does play and four others call him, that is, they also put in 50 cents. Good hands are out, it seems, making for a good pot. I'm next to last, next to the dealer. I shuffle my three cards. I look. I see an Ace of Spades. I shuffle some more. I look. I see an eight of hearts. I shuffle some more and then squeeze the cards real hard and peek. I see the tip of a red ace. I have a pair of aces. The only hand that could beat me would be a three of a kind, a rarity. I raise the bet to a dollar. Three of the remaining five players call me by putting in an additional 50 cents. This is surely one of the biggest pots of the day, I mutter to myself. I know I have the winning hand. If anybody had three of a kind, he would have raised me back. I confidently show my pair of aces and bend over to collect the pot when Googoo, a bystander because he had no money, hollers, "Cheez it! Cheez it! The cops!" Forgetting about the money, we all scrambled in every direction. When we returned to resume play, the money was gone. Googoo said, "It was a false alarm. I thought the car turning the corner was a cop's car." Googoo entered the game the next hand with my money, I'm sure. I continued playing, seething with anger, with indignation, but unable to do anything about it. He was older and too big for me, and he was Googoo. Nobody, nobody, big or small, dared challenge Googoo. He was known to be good with his fists, although I never saw him use them.

Every Sunday morning after the 10:30 Mass, we were confronted with a dilemma. Where to start the card game? If we played in the middle of Mercer Street near Allegheny Avenue, in full view of police cars cruising up and down Allegheny Avenue, we were subject to a raid anytime, depending on the cops on duty that day, or if they received any complaints from people living on Mercer Street, or from Mr. Furtek, or from churchgoers passing by. The cops would quickly turn the corner and we would scatter in four directions. Some would run down a nearby alley but that was risky. Sometimes the cops were waiting at the other end of the alley. Most would run down the length of Mercer Street and that could be risky, too, because the police car could follow you down the length of Mercer Street. Others took their chances and ran towards the cop car to Allegheny Avenue. Usually, the cops would not chase us, but you could never tell. It depended who was on duty that day. Most of the time they would simply pick up the money, hoping it was a big pot like the one Googoo took from me, tear up the cards and leave. Ten minutes later a new deck of cards would appear and we would resume playing. Sometimes, there could be as many as three or four raids on a Sunday morning, depending on who was on duty that day, how conscientious they were or how much money the cops needed that particular Sunday afternoon.

I always looked forward to Baldy entering the card game. He was easy money and he didn't seem to mind losing. His favorite expression after losing was, "Easy come, easy go." He was about a year or two older than we were, but he was a sheetmetal apprentice, working in high places like our church steeple, for example, making good money. Baldy liked to bluff. That is, he would raise the pot with nothing in his hand, hoping that everybody else would drop out. I recall one hand he raised the pot from a half-dollar to a dollar. I looked at my hand. I had a 9, 4, 2 hand. It would be hard to have a worse hand. I thought. I concentrated. I put in a dollar. I called. The other three players, who already placed in their 50 cents, dropped out, not because of Baldy's raise, but because of my call. Baldy threw his hand face down in disgust. When I showed my 9 high hand, he said, "Wait a minute." He bent over turned his cards over and showed an 8, 6, 2. The players were amazed that I called on such a low hand. I amazed myself until many years later in college, reading Edgar Allan Poe's prose works. Poe was an addicted card player. In fact, he was dismissed from West Point because of gambling. In one of his informal essays, he tried to explain this mysterious sixth sense he had while gambling that enabled him to surmise what his opponents had, almost to the point of determining what they had. I felt I had this sixth sense. The incident described above was not the only time I bet with a very poor hand and won. That is why I won so often, that is why the guys thought I was lucky, but I, like Edgar Allan Poe, attributed my winnings to my innate sixth sense. But why, then, I ask, was Poe kicked out of West Point because of his gambling debts? Why did he die destitute? Why do I continue to lose at the casinos?

48

I recall playing cards on Mercer Street one Sunday afternoon with my back facing our home about 20 yards away. I happened to turn around to see Mr. Nowacki, a friend of my parents, coming from the other end of Mercer Street, towards our home, staggering noticeably.

I never liked Mr. Nowacki whenever my family visited his family on Almond Street beyond Cleafield Street or when his family visited our home. I liked his jovial wife, always with a friendly smile and a hearty laugh, and his three attractive daughters, all a bit older than I. He, on the other hand, seemed coarse, crude, loud, who frequently became drunk quickly. He was powerfully built. His body was shaped like a gorilla, short, wide, with long, thick arms. I was hoping he would pass our home, but he didn't. He rang our doorbell. I knew Mom was home alone. I quickly dropped out of the game, even though the other players disapproved because I was quitting while winners, a no-no among gamblers. You must give your opponents an opportunity to win their money back. Nonetheless, I dropped out of the game. I followed Mr. Nowacki into our home and into our kitchen, where Mom, seeing that he was drunk, did not invite him to sit down. She stood on one side of the kitchen table, visibly nervous, he, on the other side, rocking back and forth, side to side, speaking louder than normal, occasionally turning his gaze on me. I stood in the corner near the kitchen sink. What were his intentions, I wondered, and I think my mother wondered also? Were they amorous? My mother was not an unattractive woman even at her age. Was it a pure social visit, which seemed unlikely? Finally, he got to the point of his visit. He wanted to borrow money. My mother said she didn't have any money to lend him, knowing that she would never see the money again if she did lend it to him. He wouldn't give up. He took a step closer to the kitchen table, leaned over it and raised his voice and my mother backed up a step. This time he insisted, demanded that my mother give him the money. I put my hands into my pockets and to bulk up my fists, I clutched coins in both of them and crossed them in front of me, asking myself while doing so, "Where the hell are those brass knuckles I once saw in the house?" He would not leave. He was adamant. He repeated a fourth, fifth, sixth time that he wanted money, raising his voice each time, and each time Mom said she hadn't any money. I thought, "Maybe Mom doesn't have any money. If she did, she surely would have given it to him by now." Finally, he looked at my mother and then at me. Disgustedly, he turned around and staggered out of the house. My mom just gave me a knowing look that said, "*Dzienkuje, Edziu,* for being here." "Thank you, *Edziu,* for being here." I had no fear, no fear of humiliation, during that confrontation. If he had made the slightest move to touch my mother, I would have attacked him and knew I would have beaten him to a pulp, just like Mike Kijack did to Slim Ochlak. I suppose filial love is just as strong, if not more so, than paternal love. I went back outside to resume the card playing with the coins still engraved in my palms, proud of myself. "Maybe

I'm not such a wimp, a yellow belly, after all," I thought.

49

Googoo was always trying to make an extra buck. About once a summer, he claimed he could swim out to the sand bar located in the Delaware River, directly across from the Port Richmond pier, near the New Jersey shoreline. "Who wants to bet? Any takers?" he said to a bunch of older guys standing at the corner of Mercer and Allegheny. Jimmy DiPersio was Googoo's agent, so to speak. He was drumming up bets as well, a quarter here, a dollar there. I didn't bet but I went along with the crowd. By the time we reached the pier about a quarter mile away, a group of about 50 kids and guys gathered to bet or just to watch Googoo swim out to the sandbar. Near the beginning of the pier where it met the shoreline, I remember seeing inflated prophylactics, human feces, garbage and other waste bobbing in the water. "Googoo is going to swim in this water?" I asked Socko, who was walking alongside me to the pier. But at the other end of the 100-foot pier, where Googoo would begin his quest, the water was clear and clean. With the crowd cheering him on, Googoo stripped to his shorts, waved to the crowd and dove in. He began swimming with strong, certain strokes. We watched as his bobbing blond head became smaller and smaller. Finally, after about a half-hour, he emerged from the water, stood upright and waved to us. He reached the sandbar. He rested for a few minutes, adjusted his shorts, pushed back his hair and plunged back into the water. When Googoo pulled himself up to the pier a half-hour later, he was greeted by an ovation. I don't think anybody gave it a thought as to who would pay whom if Googoo didn't make it. And Googoo probably didn't have the money to cover the bets anyway.

We younger kids idolized Googoo and the older guys his age admired him, despite his shenanigans, and some feared him. One day Googoo was suddenly gone. Googoo joined the Marines. Some said it was not of his own volition, but a judge told him to join the Marines or go to jail for something he did. We all missed him when one day he came home after basic training, trimmer, tanner, handsomer than ever and when he walked by in his blue and white dress uniform on his way to the nine o'clock Mass (I never recalled any other time Googoo going to church.), we were in awe of him.

I was still in awe of him when I met him many years later in Pilsudski Social Club where my brother Joe took me to show off his younger brother, Wimpy, now a priest. Googoo was at the bar. It was the first time we had seen each other in twenty years. He bought me a beer, and we reminisced for a few minutes about the old days, but he couldn't stay; he was on his way home. Googoo was now a settled married man with a family, driving a truck for his father-in-law. I was surprised. I was saddened to hear a few years later that Googoo died of cancer. I never thought that Googoo would ever settle down or that he would ever die—at least not so soon.

50

One reason I didn't enjoy going to Maxie Shapiro's produce store just up the street on the corner of Mercer Street and Allegheny Avenue was that my mother would tell me in Polish what she wanted and Maxie often didn't know what that was. He would give me what he thought my mother wanted. I would bring it home; it would be the wrong item, and I would have to return it. Sometimes I did this two or three times; I'd be getting more embarrassed each time as I tried to explain to Maxie what my mother wanted and Maxie would be getting more exasperated.

Maxie was one of the few Jewish merchants in the neighborhood. He was about 4'10" and weighed about 160 pounds. He always wore the same dirty fedora and a dirty white apron, bloodstained from the chickens he killed in the back of his store. He shaved only once a week, on Sunday, when he went to a downtown Philadelphia businessmen's "club" to relax: to get a massage, a Turkish bath, a nice dinner and some other relaxation, as he hinted to me one day much later. He deserved it. (I mean everything but the "other relaxation.") He, along with his wife, a clean, quiet, dignified, handsome woman, about a foot taller than Maxie, worked hard the other six days. Early every morning he would bring out bushel baskets of fruits and vegetables and display them strategically in front of the store. And almost every day one or more of us, or a gang of us, would walk by and when he wasn't looking, snitch an apple, a pear, an orange. Sometimes he would see us, and it would be a funny sight to see Maxie running down Mercer Street or across Allegheny Avenue, trying to catch us, he in his forties or early fifties, with a footspan of about two feet, trying to catch us in our teens with a footspan of about five feet. Sometimes one of us deliberately stole a piece of fruit just for the fun of watching Maxie chase the thief down Mercer Street or across Allegheny Avenue.

The Shapiros had two children, Claire and Joseph. Claire was short like her father, with creamy white complexioned skin, offset by dark eyes and dark hair, with full, luscious lips and a beautifully contoured mature bosom. We often stood on the corner of Mercer and Allegheny Avenue and watched her walk home from the 60 trolley car from school, with school books shielding that bosom. Joseph? I never paid much attention to him—except I remember that he was tall, thin, with sandy-colored curly hair and he was very aloof. He never spoke to us as he walked by us from the trolley car on his way from some private school somewhere in Philadephia, or Central High, known as an excellent public school in Philadelphia with a heavily Jewish enrollment. What they did for social life, I don't know. They never associated with us. Claire never acknowledged our whistles and suggestive remarks, but I think she secretly enjoyed them. As far as we could see, they never left their home except to go to school. They didn't have a car. Nobody seemed to visit them. They appeared to live in total isolation, except for Claire and Joseph going to school, and Maxie going to his Sunday trip to his businessmen's club.

And these two proper children and mother had to live above the stench that emanated from the store below, particularly the chicken store in the rear of the produce store. We neighbors could smell the stench half way down the block on many occasions, especially during hot summer days when the breeze was going north up Mercer Street. The immediate neighbors, who included our family, complained of rats that we claimed came from Maxie's store. We reported him to the Board of Health but with little success..

Recently, I read a disturbing article in the March 12, 2001, issue of *The New Yorker* magazine. It was about the frequent pogroms against the Jews conducted by the Poles of Jedwabne, a city a few miles from where my father was born in Karwowa. The persecutions of the Jews by the Poles ended, according to *The New Yorker* account, with the burning to death 1,600 of them, about half the population of Jedwabne, in a barn. My wife and I briefly visited Jedwabne in November of 1999 and we would have inquired about this tragic event had we known about it at the time. (Today, I received an Easter Card from my cousin Stan, postmarked Jedwabne.) There must have been strong anti-Semitic sentiment in that region of Poland. Was my father tinged with it when he grew up there? I think so from the remarks he would make when we had visitors. He did say, with some resentment, that Jews owned most of the businesses in Poland, that they were shrewd businessmen and that they would succeed because Jews helped one another while Poles would not succeed because they would not patronize another Pole because Poles were jealous of fellow Poles and did not want to see them get ahead.

Were there any anti-Semitic motives behind our treatment of Maxie Shapiro and his family? I don't think so. We teased Mr. Furtek, a Pole, as much as we teased Maxie. In fact, we liked Maxie; we liked to tease him. We never said anything disparaging to him or about him. But I must confess that when I got older and a bit more introspective that I detected some anti-Semitic feelings in me. Did they come from my father? Did they come from my Roman Catholic upbringing, from my seminary training? I don't know. I know it presented a problem to me when after leaving the priesthood and writing for the *Buffalo News,* I was covering a talk given by a Jewish scholar from Chicago who was involved in trying to improve the relations between Christians and Jews. The topic of her talk was the Polish Roman Catholic Church's efforts to found a convent outside Auschwitz. The speaker opposed building the convent at Auschwitz and opposed the Poles acting as victims in the tragedy of Auschwitz. She strongly suggested that the Poles shared in the guilt of what happened at Auschwitz. The annual talk was sponsored by a Jewish couple in Niagara Falls and was held at Niagara University in nearby Lewiston.

Most of the audience of about 300 were Jewish, I surmised, from the hearty laughter the speaker received when she ridiculed the Poles. I had to control myself; I told myself to put aside my feelings, to report this talk as objectively as possible. I worked harder and longer than usual on my summation of the highlights of her talk and I thought I did a good job. At least the editor did not edit it much. I thought it was a positive, thorough, fair summary of her talk. I deliberately did not mention the anti-Pole sentiment that I detected in her talk. But the paper received a letter from the woman a few days after my article appeared, complaining that I misrepresented her, on what I thought, was a very minor point, not worthy of a rejoinder on my part. I think it was my Polish name in the byline that triggered her complaint. Am I anti-Semitic today? Not consciously. Unconsciously? Possibly, but every time this prejudice tries to rear its ugly head, I try hard to eradicate it before it surfaces. It's un-Christian, unnatural, inhumane to be anti-Semitic, and, of course, I shudder at the mere thought of the Holocaust. But I'm afraid I must admit that deep deep down, uncontrollably, like a primal urge, I do harbor anti-Semitic feelings. Yet, it brings to mind a highly unusual, I think, incident that occurred during the early days of my priesthood. I befriended this Jewish fellow, Harry. One day I was having a drink with him at the bar in his bowling alley. Out of the blue he asked me to hear his confession. He said he had something that was bothering him. He was not a Catholic but I offered to hear his confession at the bar and give him absolution then and there, privately, quietly, if it would make him feel better. He said no. He wanted me to hear his confession in a confessional. We went to the school's chapel nearby and I heard his confession in the confessional there. He sat in the chapel for a few minutes afterward. Was it a sacramental confession? I doubt it. But that's beside the point. He felt immeasurably better, and we continued to be fast friends until his death a few years afterwards. I recall, too, again early in my priesthood, attending in a synagogue, a sparsely attended lecture by Archbishop Joseph Bernardin, who at the time was the Bishop of Cincinnatti, on Christian-Jewish relations when such lectures were not so fashionable, when the Jews were still called "perfidious" in the Holy Week liturgy of the Roman Catholic Church.

My wife and I intended to visit Auschwitz when we visited Cracow, Poland, in the fall of 1999. We were dissuaded from doing so by a young Irishman we met in Bialystok, (A well-known name today. Max Bialystock is the name of the leading character in the hit musical, *The Producers.*) a city in northeast Poland near the Russian border. He said, "Auschwitz is very, very depressing. Go instead to the city of Zakopata in the Tatra Mountains. The scenery is out of this world." Zakopata is in the southernmost part of Poland near Slovakia. Visiting Zakopata was a disappointment because it was the "dead" season. All the lifts to scenic views were closed for the season. We wished we had gone to Auschwitz instead, no matter how depressing.

If we as kids growing up in Port Richmond weren't consciously anti-Semitic, we were certainly consciously anti-German because of the war. The whole neighborhood heaped scorn on a German single mother and her son, Rudy. He was our age and they lived next to Borkowski's Delicatessen on the other side of Allegheny Avenue across from Majeski's Delicatessan. We never invited him to join in with our activities. In fact, we openly and publicly scorned him and called him derogatory names that I don't recall now. I don't know whether our ostracism of him bothered him that much but it must have. We heard when he was in high school that he was deeply involved in scientific projects in the basement of his home. I don't think they had anything to do with the making of the atom bomb.

51

In addition to running errands to Radzikowski's store, another chore I didn't mind doing was mopping the linoleum kitchen floor on Saturday mornings because most Saturdays Mom would give me a dime to see the Saturday matinee movies at the Richmond Street Theater. That was the highlight of my week, and the highlight of every boy my age. After cursorily and quickly mopping the floor and after getting the dime from my mother, I would run out of the house to meet some friends and scurry on to the Richmond Movies, four short blocks east on Allegheny Avenue and a long block south on Richmond Street.

We never cared what the main feature was. Often, there wasn't any, just a number of shorts, which was fine with us: cartoons, Robert Benchley 15 minute comedy shorts (whose humor we never appreciated), special features, the weekly summary of news, called Pathe News that was introduced by Robert Trout's youthful, mellifluous voice as a weathervane rooster crowed as it turned, and the Chapter, as we called it, the weekly serial for which we really went to the movies on Saturday afternoon. Each week for twelve continuous weeks we would leave the theater wondering how our hero, usually a cowboy pursued by Indians, would avoid certain death as his wagon went hurtling over the cliff. And next week we would feel duped when, unbelievably, we would see our hero jump out of the wagon just before it went hurtling over the cliff. "Didn't you see him go over the cliff last week?" "Yeah! Sure!" But each week for 12 straight weeks we would come back for next week's chapter, only to be duped again. We were so gullible at that age. And we tried not to miss the Last Chapter when the final resolution would take place, when good would triumph over evil, when our hero would finally be triumphant. And then the next week another Chapter of another serial would begin: Flash Gordon, starring Buster Crabbe; Tarzan, starring Johnny Weismuller, the Olympic swimming hero; Fu Manchu, the sinister Chinese warlord; Charlie Chan, a Chinese super sleuth with his sidekick son; and Tom Mix, Buck Rogers, Hopalong Cassidy, Ken Maynard, Wild Bill Elliot, Johnny Mack Brown, the former football player, the Lone Ranger, all cowboy stalwarts, all our heroes.

There was more to the Saturday movies than just going to see the weekly chapter. If Mom felt generous or if I coaxed her enough, she would give me an extra penny to buy a huge, fresh, soft pretzel to munch on during the movies. There was also the throwing of paper planes, half-eaten pretzels and fruit at the screen, enjoying how the objects glistened in the beams from the projector or as they smashed against the silver screen. And there were the catcalls when the villain was beating on the hero; laughter of a humorous remark from the audience at a serious moment in the movie; nervous laughter, giggles and whistles at romantic kissing scenes.

I didn't get a dime every Saturday. Maybe I refused to clean the linoleum kitchen floor; maybe I was bad; maybe Mom didn't have the dime or needed it for something else. In that case those of us who didn't have the price of admission would all pitch in with what money we had to pay for the admission of one of the gang. It was his job as soon as the house lights went out to open slightly one of the pre-arranged side fire-exit doors. When he did so, on all fours, we would quickly "sneak" in and, hidden by the seats, scatter throughout the theater before the manager noticed the light coming from the open door.

This method of sneaking in was so successful and so easy that we used it even when we had the price of admission. One time, however, we waited for the door to open, and it did not open. Afterward, we saw Reds, who was to open the door, and angrily asked him, "What happened?" He said, "The manager stood by the door. I couldn't open the door." We had no way of knowing whether that was the case, but we sometimes thought that once he was in with our money he forgot about us. Eventually, this happened more often than not so we resumed paying our way in if we had the money.

We ate soft pretzels not only when we were going to the movies but anywhere, anytime. It was our staple when we were growing up. Pushcarts filled with pretzels rolled down the streets. Red four-wheeled children's wagons, piled high with pretzels, were pulled through the neighborhoods or stationed at street corners and at busy intersections, at trolley car and elevated train stops, at newspaper stands, in corner grocery stores. They were hawked at roadsides to motorists waiting for the traffic light to change. Grown men supported families, sent their children to college on what they earned selling pretzels. And just until a few years ago, the first thing my wife and I would do when we arrived in Philadephia, and the last thing we would do as we left Philadelphia, was to stop at a roadside cart for a bag of six pretzels for a quarter. (Now in Buffalo they sell for more than a dollar apiece.) After so many years of selling pretzels this way, the city has banned the practice for hygienic reasons: The man standing on a corner in cold weather had to relieve himself: how and where did he do so?

How did he wash his hands? Back then we never gave a thought to how he washed his hands.

I lived on pretzels during my four years of high school. I remember mountains and mountains of pretzels spilling over the table in the kitchen of the school cafeteria. Most days that was my lunch: pretzels, penny a piece, six for a nickel, with plenty of mustard. Today, every grocery store, every convenience store, every supermarket still sells soft pretzels in Philadelphia and now in Buffalo, in Lockport, in Niagara Falls Malls. In fact, to this day, I can't pass a soft-pretzel concession in a mall without buying one even though it bothers me to pay a dollar for something I paid a penny for in my childhood.

There were other neighborhood theaters we attended as we got older and wiser and no longer taken in by the phony weekly serials or chapters. There was the Clearfield Theater, at Clearfield and Belgrade Streets: a smaller but nicer movie house than the Richmond. Then a few blocks south at Belgrade and Auburn Streets was a new movie house, appropriately named the Belgrade. It was tiny in comparison to the Richmond and showed movies more for adults and sometimes movies in Polish dialogue. One year my mother went faithfully every Tuesday night, regardless of the movie, English, Polish, adult, children, because that was dish night, when everybody received a free dish toward a set of dishes. Once in a while my mother couldn't make it and rather than interrupt the set she would tell me to go. I went gladly. Adult picture or no adult picture, English or no English. It didn't matter. A movie was a movie then. Of course, there was no television.

52

Being sent by my mother to the Belgrade Movies on a Tuesday night to get a dish had a powerful, life-changing effect on my life, I think. A young, friendly, attractive girl in her late 20s and her mother moved into Mercer Street. She always had a friendly hello to us standing on the corner on her way home from work on the 60 trolley. On occasion, she would even pause to say more than hello. She would try to engage us in some form of conversation. One day, probably in an effort to civilize us a little, she stopped and asked if we would like to learn how to dance. She would be willing to teach us. Beerzy speaking for all of us said, "Sure. Why not?" "Okay. I'll see you at my house tomorrow at 7." None of us, all in our teens, knew how to dance. It was frustrating and embarrassing not to dance at a dance, to just stand against the wall, making salacious comments at the girls and ridiculing the boys who did dance. This invitation to learn how to dance was a golden opportunity and we couldn't wait till tomorrow night. Just as I was going to meet the guys on the corner to go over her house, my mother said, "Edziu, I can't go to the Belgrade tonight. I want you to go to get this dish, the last one in the set." "But, Mom, I have somewhere important to go." "No, I want you to go and get that dish." So I went to the Belgrade and missed the dance lesson.

The next day I asked, "How did things go?" "Great," said Beerzy.

"She was really good. She taught us the jitterbug and the box-step slow dance. I can't wait to use them this Saturday at St. Al's Dance." I went to the dance. I stood around and watched as everyone else danced the night away. I went through high school not knowing how to dance. That's why I never went to the proms. And that's possibly another reason why I went to the seminary. At least I think it was a contributing factor and I think it was a contributing factor to my leaving the priesthood. All during my priesthood I longed to dance. Whenever I attended a festive gathering such as a wedding reception or a school or parish activity, I wanted to get up and dance, especially the Polka. In the beginning of my priesthood I don't think it was acceptable for a priest to dance; later, it was acceptable but I didn't know how. Also, while I'm on the topic, I'm not certain my marriage to Shirley is valid because she said, half seriiously, that she would not marry me unless I learned to dance, which I promptly and gladly did.

53

Then, as we got older, in our early teens, we branched outside the Port Richmond neighborhood theaters: to the Allegheny Theater at Frankford and Allegheny Avenues, about a half mile west of Richmond; to the Midway at Kensington and Allegheny Avenues, another quarter of a mile to the west, and to the Iris, just around the corner from the Midway on Kensington Avenue. In these theaters outside of Port Richmond, we were mixing with the big world, with kids from other neighborhoods, from other nationalities, from other races.

The Midway was a splendid, elegant movie house. It was a treat for us just to enter it. After you paid your admission, you walked into a wide and deep lobby with mirrors on the wall, plush red sofas to sit on, paintings to gaze at, ornate chandeliers, deep, red, plush carpets. As you entered you were faced with a wide, magnificent circular staircase on the left that led to the balcony. The Midway did not run the serials, the cartoons, the second rate B movies of the Richmond Theater. It ran first-rate adult movies. In fact, one of the last movies I remember seeing at the Midway was the memorable "Gone With the Wind" in 1939 when it first came out. I was ten at the time. The Midway was a fitting venue for that movie.

The only problem with the Midway was it was too expensive. Sometimes, if we wanted to see a movie at the Midway badly enough, we would pick up a few rags from home, walk to K and A and start polishing cars as they waited for the long light to turn at the K and A intersection. Most of the time, the drivers were more annoyed than anything at our boldness to start polishing their cars without their consent.. Sometimes, however, they tipped us a nickel, a dime or quarter, not so much for the shine, but for our initiative, our entrepreneurship. Sometimes we made enough to go to the Midway and to the Horn & Hardart Automat Cafeteria next door. The Horn & Hardart was a clean, spacious restaurant with dozens of tables. Along one entire wall were windowed cubicles with different foods in them. Some had sandwiches; others had desserts, fruits, etc. You placed the necessary amount of money in the slot, the window to the cubicle would open and you would take out what was in it. This was intriguing back then but, of course, today it is commonplace because most food machines work on the same principle. That was a special day, a rare treat, to be able to go to the Midway and then to Horn & Hardart. Even if we didn't have enough money to buy anything at Horn & Hardart, we often went in just to walk down the length of the air-conditioned cafeteria and to gawk at all the different, delicious looking foods and to drink their cool water out of nice, clean glasses stacked high next to the water cooler.

The Allegheny Theater was an old, large, majestic, magnificent structure built originally for live performances. The ceiling was so high that you couldn't make out the decorations that adorned the ceiling. A towering, resplendent chandelier dangled from the highest point of the ceiling. The theater had a balcony in the back that extended over almost half of

the orchestra. On both sides of the theater were a series
of alcove-like box seats protruding over the orchestra
and each succeeding one slightly higher than the
previous one. Of course, the entire theater was
carpeted with deep plush carpets. The seats were cloth-
lined and cushioned; the walls had drapes; the stage
was cavernous, extending from side to side and deep
towards the back of the theater. It was what I thought
an opera house would look like. It still held live
performances occasionally on a Saturday afternoon: a
variety show, a talent show, a vaudeville show.

I remember I went alone on a Saturday afternoon to
the Allegheny Theater to see a movie. I enjoyed it so
much that to see the movie a second time I hid under
the seats as everybody filed out. Unfortunately, I
forgot that I had to be home by five o'clock to go with
the family to a wedding in the country. When I realized
halfway through the second performance where I was
supposed to be, I jumped out of my seat, ran out of the
theater and started running down Allegheny Avenue,
hoping and praying I wasn't too late. Just as I reached

the Northeastern Hospital at Chatham and Allegheny Avenue, a red chow dog suddenly appeared from between two parked cars and bit me on my left thigh, ripping my pants and drawing blood. More frightened than anything. I began to cry and scream loudly. A Good Samaritan picked me up, ran across Allegheny Avenue to the hospital's emergency room. Still more frightened than anything, I was still crying. I probably was inoculated with a rabies preventative drug and maybe given a sedative. The small wound was dressed with a small bandage. I finally calmed down, gave the nurse my name and address and was told to go home. I knew I was too late to go to the wedding. The whole family was gone but the front door of the house was unlocked. I waited with trepidation for my father to return home. I finally fell asleep on the sofa. The next day I merely told my father that I forgot about the wedding and he accepted my explanation.

The following Monday I was playing on Mercer Street when I noticed a woman with a leather bag in her hand knock at our door. I hid behind a parked car until I noticed that after a few minutes she left. What I could gather from my mother was that it was a nurse from the hospital who wanted to see me about something. I never told anyone about being bit by a dog for fear of being punished.

There was another time I hid when I was playing outdoors and saw somebody approach our door. A gentleman with a speckled horse and camera came to Mercer Street, inviting all the kids to put on a cowboy hat, a vest, chaps and cap gun holster, and to mount the horse to have our picture taken. All we had to do was give him our name and address. I just wanted to sit on a real live horse, not like the wooden horses of the merry-go-round, so I got dressed in the cowboy paraphernalia and was hoisted on to the pony to have my picture taken. About a week later, the man appeared at our door as I was playing outside. I dared not go home for fear my mother would scold me for having my picture taken without her permission. When I finally did go home after the gentleman left, my mother said, "There was a nice man here a while ago selling pictures of children on a horse. He had a nice picture of a boy that looked like you. I wanted to buy it but I wasn't sure it was you so I didn't buy it." I was so disappointed. I wanted Mom to buy it too. I didn't tell her it was me and I let it go at that.

54

Each year a carnival would come to our neighborhood. But this year the circus came to town, to our neighborhood and put down stakes at Aramingo Avenue from Westmoreland Street all the way to Ontario Street, which at that time, was a spacious empty lot. Today, that block is part of the busiest section in all of Port Richmond.

The circus was a big, big event and the price of admission indicated as much: 50 cents for children, way out of our price range. Beerzy and I reconnoitered the situation; in other words, how to find a way to sneak in. We felt we could sneak into almost anything if we put our minds to it. But this circus seemed impregnable. A 10-foot high temporary fence encircled the entire circus. The tents were fastened tight to the ground with no chance of lifting the canvas to sneak under. And even if we did scale the fence and did sneak under a tent, we didn't know what we were sneaking into. It would be just our luck to sneak into the main tent with hundreds of spectators watching us. Or it could be where they kept wild animals. Carnivals we could handle, but a circus? Beerzy and I weren't sure. We were stumped. Beerzy had an idea: "I know a place where we can sell light bulbs for a nickel apiece and I know where we can get the light bulbs." "Where?" I asked eagerly. "The Allegheny Movies. Did you notice on each landing of the fire escape there are 2 blue light bulbs?" "Yeah! Great idea! Let's go!" I said.

We decided to start at the top landing first and work our way down. I lifted Beerzy up; he unscrewed the bulbs and put them in a shopping bag. We were so intent on unscrewing the light bulbs that we didn't notice the manager at the ground level of the fire escape. "All right, boys, come on down," he hollered up to us. We were caught; there was no where to go. As we slowly walked down, we paused at a landing. We evaluated our chances of escape. We could possibly jump off the fire escape landing to the roof of the building next to the theater. We looked at the length of the jump, about five feet. Possibly, we could make it. We looked down at the ground if we didn't make the jump: about a 50-foot fall. We looked at each other, shook our heads; we'll take our chances with getting caught. Maybe the manager will let us off, we hoped, and continued walking slowly down into the custody of the manager and two ushers.

Once we were in the manager's office, he said, "You kids have been stealing these light bulbs for months." (The idea was not original with Beerzy, apparently.) "I have to set an example. I'm locking you up." "Locking us up!" We didn't expect that harsh a punishment. We probably would have chanced jumping from the fire escape if we had known that. The paddy wagon arrived a few minutes later, just as the theater was letting out; the lobby of the theater and the front steps were filled with people, wanting to know what was happening, who was being arrested and for what. Out walked these two frightened kids, between two burly policemen. (No, we were not handcuffed; no, there were no flashbulbs popping).

With two policemen in the cab of the patrol wagon and two sitting in the wagon with us, we were taken to the 24th Police Precinct at Belgrade and Clearfield Streets, next door to the Clearfield Theater. "At least we're getting a free ride home," I said to Beerzy. Beerzy said, "This is better than the 'Dead End Kids,' Wimp," alluding to a popular movie at the time about a group of tough kids from a tough New York City neighborhood. They were our heroes after whom we patterned our lives. We were fingerprinted (we must have been all of 12 or 13), all for effect, I hope. The desk-sergeant asked: "What's your names? Where do you live? What's your phone numbers?" "We don't have a phone," we answered in unison." The sergeant paused, scratched his head. "Take them home."

We were placed in the backseat of a patrol car and delivered home. First, to Beerzy's home on Mercer Street on the other side of Allegheny Avenue and then to mine. Neighbors congregated in front of our home, wondering why a police car came to our home. Fortunately, my father was not home. It was Saturday afternoon and Pop was, as often was the case, at the Royal Café across Allegheny Avenue, far enough away not to notice the police car at his home. The police officer explained to my mother what happened. Luckily, she didn't understand a word he said, I'm sure. I then told Mom my version of what happened which was that we were lost, and the police were returning us home. I'm not sure she believed me. My father came home drunk that night, and my mother was more upset with him than with me and she never told him about my being brought home by the police. There was another shellacking I fully expected to get from my father and never did. When I look back at my childhood, I think the times I feared being punished by my father far exceeded the actual times he did physically punish me.

55

My mother didn't have much of a social life but she made the most of what little she had. During the nice weather months on Saturday mornings, she would socialize with neighbors as they washed the front steps and pavements in front of their homes. It was a ritual I enjoyed watching from the front window. Mom would have a bucket of hot soapy water, with a scrub brush and rag in it, and a broom. She would spill some water over the steps, scrub them down, and rinse them with the rag. She would then splash the excess water over the pavement and tell me to get a bucket of clear water and with the broom she would wash down the pavement and sweep the excess water down the gutter to the inlet at the end of the street. All the while, she would be gossiping and talking with the neighbors.

On Sunday morning, she would get all dressed up for the 12 o'clock Solemn High Mass. During the winter months, every Sunday she wore the same black shoes, the same black dress, the same black coat with a fake black fur collar and a large rimmed black hat with a black feather sticking out of it and a shiny, black imitation leather handbag draped around her arm. On summer Sundays, my mother wore the same white shoes, the same light blue dress and the same small white hat with a small white handbag. I don't know how my mother smudged her white shoes (probably in the rush to receive Holy Communion), but about every other Saturday in the backyard I had to polish her shoes with white Ace Polish. It was a delicate job that Mom was particular about. I had to be careful not to put any of the white polish on the sides of the soles or on the heels and I wasn't supposed to streak the polish. Sometimes I had to do the shoes over again if I left streaks on them. I enjoyed watching my mother put on her hat and primping her hair before the mirror in the living room downstairs as she was about to leave the house for church— always alone.

Occasionally, she would have neighborhood girl friends, Mrs. Murawska, Mrs. Majka down the street, pop in for a brief visit. Sometimes, Mom would visit her long-time friend from the Old Country, dying from tuberculosis, Mrs. Paczynska from Tilton Street. Mrs. Paczynska was my godmother, and if Mom were on her way to visit with Mrs. Paczynska and saw me playing out on the street, she would call me over, take out her handkerchief, put spittle on it and wash my face (How I hated the smell of the spittle!) and then drag me along to visit with Mrs. Paczynski which consisted of my sitting alone in this darkened room as she and Mom visited. It was so boring I could have screamed.

When I was about ten, I sensed my mother's loneliness, surrounded by insensitive males; how unappreciated, how taken for granted she was, how overworked she was. (After visiting Poland recently, I would have to say conditions weren't that bad in this country for Polish immigrants 60 70 years ago.) Mom would be on her feet for hours ironing the shirts of my three older brothers and father. I remember her pleading with my three older brothers to wear a dress shirt at least twice before throwing it in the laundry basket. It seemed she spent all day Tuesday just ironing shirts. I would give her a break by ironing the handkerchiefs as she sat down to rest. But she wouldn't trust me with the regular hankies, only those that were converted sugar bags, which I never enjoyed using. They were rough on the nose.

I would help out by running errands for her. I often would run to the corner grocery store to get something that she needed for supper. I didn't mind going to the small Polish grocery store, Radzikowskis, on Madison Street down the other end of our Mercer Street. I knew they would know what my mother wanted and I rather enjoyed bounding over the neighbors' steps to get there and I couldn't lose any money because I didn't need any money—just the small, tattered, food account book.

I also remember being bathed by my mother in the kitchen in front of the stove, the only warm room in the house. After a snowstorm, I remember my mother being distressed when she ruined several pairs of our shoes when she placed them in the stove to dry out faster. The soles curled up so much that the shoes couldn't be worn again. I remember being sent down to the cellar, it seemed hourly, by my mother to shovel coke into the furnace. After a while this became boring. Rather than walk the full length of the cellar and carefully place the shovel into the furnace, to make it more challenging, I would open wide the furnace door and fling the coke from one end of the cellar to the other, just like I saw it done in the movies, in factory scenes, in ship scenes, in train scenes. The only problem is that I more often than not missed the furnace opening. Mom in the kitchen could tell from the sound of the coke spilling all over the floor what I was doing, and she would holler down to stop throwing coke at the furnace and to pick up the coke scattered all over the cellar floor.

It was a milestone event in our house when Pop bought a gas heater and had ducts extended through every room in the house. It was a luxury to go to bed at night and get up in the morning to a warm bedroom. And I didn't have to shovel coke anymore.

56

Throughout this memoir I have used an abundance of nicknames. That's because practically everyone in our neighborhood was known by a nickname. The origin of some of these nicknames are traceable, others are not. I know, for example, when and why I was nicknamed Wimpy. There was this greasy spoon restaurant, Pep's, near the corner of Richmond and Allegheny Avenue that I have already referred to several times. During the summer months, Pep's opened the front window and served hamburgers and hotdogs to outside customers. There were about six of us that evening. We all lined up single file to place our order. Everybody ordered a hotdog. When I ordered a hamburger, probably because my mother made such good hamburgers, the gang all turned in unison and Sajo called out: "Wimpy," a fat character with a funny hat and small mustache in the Popeye comics whose shirt button popped every time he ate a hamburger, while Popeye, with bursting biceps, threw down a can of spinach. The name has stuck to this very day. Even during my priesthood, I was called Father Wimpy by my childhood buddies. I never minded the nickname until later when it dawned on me what its shortened version meant.

I don't know why we called Ray Radomiolii, Beerzy, unless he was seen drinking a beer early in life or his stomach protruded after a big meal like a beer belly, which he now has, the last time I saw him. We called Frank Pijanowski, Socko because he was small and stocky like the comic character. Socko doesn't figure much in these memoirs but he was a big part of my youth who ended tragically, I think. Socko was short about 4'11", whatever was the minimum height to join the United States Marines. Socko was always extremely self-conscious about his height or lack of it. One of the reasons was, I'm sure, he was often kidded about how convenient it was to be that short whenever he slow danced with a taller girl, which was often the case. Socko wanted desperately to join the Marines and we were all surprised when they accepted him. By the time he was discharged, I was in the seminary and would visit him and his parents when I got home for a two-week summer vacation. After ordination I found out that Socko was no longer working at the carpet factory and never left the house except to go to Sunday Mass. In the next few years, both his parents died and I heard that Socko had become a total recluse, never leaving the house, even for Sunday Mass. His two sisters, who lived in New Jersey, were looking after him, I heard. Now home on vacation as a priest I wanted to visit him but, regretfully, I did not, fearing what I would encounter because nobody, except his two sisters, had seen Socko for several years. I heard later that year he was found dead in his home by one of his sisters. If he had been able to overcome his complex about his height, or if he had found a nice girl his height, he would be alive today because he was a fitness buff in his early years, and he was a great kid with wonderful parents and two caring sisters.

We called Walt Krupa, Baldy, because he was prematurely bald at age 10. I saw Baldy and his family not too long ago and he is still prematurely bald—the same as he was 50 years ago. Baldy should have been a long distance runner. I recall one evening standing around Mercer and Allegheny that he boasted he could run around the park, a full city block, 25 times without stopping. At this time, Baldy, a short, slight figure was about 13 years old, already smoking for a few years. We doubted he could. "I'll betcha," he said. I remember betting a quarter that he couldn't. We all went to the park and watched intently as Baldy started out at a brisk pace and maintained that pace until the 25th lap when he sprinted the entire lap, and ended without even breathing hard.

I remember, too, the time Baldy stole a rug from the same carpet factory Socko worked in. It was not exactly the perfect crime. The day Baldy decided to swipe the rug, he wore to work his older brother's overcoat that hung below his knees. Before leaving work that day Baldy rolled the rug around his body, tied it with rope and put on the overcoat. He walked out of the factory rather stiffly but undetected, with the usual busy crowd rushing to catch the 60 trolley eager to get home. But Baldy ran into trouble when he tried to board the high boarding step of the 60 trolley. Baldy couldn't bend his knees because of the rug wrapped around them. He tried gamely several times. The conductor became impatient as Baldy vainly tried again to board the trolley. Finally, in full view of everybody, Baldy unbuttoned his coat, unwrapped the rug, re-rolled it and boarded the crowded 60 trolley, carrying the rug under his arm, to everybody's hilarious enjoyment and Baldy's extreme embarrassment.

We probably called Raymond Kolek, Sammy, after the Negro character Sambo because of his dark complexion. I don't know why we called Joe Gmerek, Tom Mix, or his brother Chet, Dillo, other than Joe might have been a Tom Mix fan and Chet might have liked dill pickles. It was obvious why we called Joe Bednarek, Bedbugs, or Al Przesztelski, Pretzels. I know why we called Walt Kapusta, Cabbo, because *kapusta* means cabbage in Polish. I don't know why we called Leonard Gniewek, Beebo, other than it might have had something to do with his amazing athletic prowess. He was quick as a bee or as accurate and swift as a BB, used in air rifles. But it certainly was in our time the most recognized nickname in Port Richmond with Joe Majeski's enigmatic Googoo, a close second. Maybe Joe was called Googoo because of his good looks or because the girls went gaga over him. I know why we called Gene Dipersio, Chubby; of course, he was chubby, and his brother Jimmy DiPersio, we called Dipersio, probably the least creative of our nicknames. I don't know why we called Henry Growniak, Huntzy; other than he had rounded shoulders like the Hunchback of Notre Dame, a popular film at the time. I know why we called Joe Groch, Beansy, because *groch* in Polish means beans. I know why we called Alfie Borowniak Rusty, because of his flaming reddish hair. I know why they called my oldest brother Crany because Joe pronounced his last name Chrzanowski, Kranoski while I pronounce it Kryzanowski. In Polish, it is pronounced Kszanovski.

They called my next oldest brother Stan Tiger because he was a tiger when he fought in Furtek's driveway, especially against Joe "Bedbugs" Bednarik. They called my next oldest brother Walt Tarzan because of his physique and good looks, except he was better looking than Johnny Weismuller.

We called Edward Haber, Reds, obviously, because of his reddish blond hair that he used to have and fair complexion. We called Frank Kutrzyka, Corpo, possibly because his last name began with the k sound. We called Ed Sajecki, Sajo, obviously a take-off his surname. We called Johnny Bujak, Booj, a shortened version of his surname. We called Walt Moleski, whose father was a prominent doctor in Port Richmond, Mo. We called Frank Marciniak, Chiseler, because he had a chisel-like chin. We called Frank Radomicki, Beerzy's older brother, Shooey, because he was fleet of foot, I think. We called Charley Radomicki, Beerzy's oldest brother, Big Charlie because he was big. These are just a sampling of nicknames found within a four-to six-block area

Ed Chrzanowski

centered around Mercer and Allegheny during the '30s and '40s. I probably have forgotten as many as I have remembered.

57

The following summer, now that we were 16 years old, Corpo, Beerzy, Sajo and I got a job at Atlas Casket Co in the neighborhood at Tulip Street near Allegheny Avenue. We started at 60 cents an hour, the minimum wage then. We were assigned difficult, technical, somewhat dangerous jobs; for example, sawing wood with a powerful electrical overhead saw for the wooden caskets; cutting and bending the metal to make the sides and bottom of the metal caskets; putting together wooden frames to place the caskets in, and other jobs. The foreman kept us busy all the time. Corpo, Beerzy, and Sajo talked it over and decided to strike for higher wages. The strike lasted about an hour. They were promptly fired. I stayed on for the remainder of the summer, and I think they regarded me as a "scab" for not going out on strike with them but they never consulted me. The only thing I enjoyed about that job were the occasional times I went with the driver to deliver caskets to Delaware and to

Maryland. Sometimes I would sit on the caskets in the back of the open-air truck and enjoy the countryside. I would help the driver unload a casket here, a five-minute job, and move on to another place to unload a casket or two there, maybe 20, 30 miles away for another five minutes of work. That kind of work I enjoyed.

I didn't work my senior year of high school. It seemed like I worked all the time ever since I was 12 years old when I started setting pins at the Polish American Club. I thought I deserved a rest my final year of high school. And, anyway, I might be going into the seminary next year. After graduation from high school, however, I thought I better help pay for the clothes I had to buy for the seminary, principally, a black suit and a cassock, so I got a job at Spruance Paint Co., located in the neighborhood at Richmond and Ontario Streets. I applied with another fellow, also a recent high school graduate. The hiring person asked if we took chemistry and physics lab courses in high school. I said yes; the other fellow said no. The hiring person placed me in an air-conditioned lab to test the viscosity of the paints they were in the process of making. The other fellow was assigned to work under the boiling sun in the yard rolling 50 gallon drums of paint around. Later when I taught, I often used this experience as a small example of how academic courses can get you better jobs. During my lunch hours I recall memorizing the Latin conjugation and declension endings, preparing myself for entrance to the seminary. On July 16, I quit Spruance, which was pre-arranged with them, and the next day, without any fanfare, I kissed my mother and father goodbye and Joe and Walt drove me to the North Philadelphia train station on Broad Street and Glenwood Avenue, near Allegheny Avenue, to catch the train for the seminary.

St. Adalbert's school picture, 1939, age nine.

58

But I'm getting ahead of myself. There are a few things to write about my elementary schooling, about my sandlot football career and about my high school days.

I still remember vividly my first day of school because a nun slapped me hard across the face. St. Adalbert's Elementary School is run by the Sisters of the Holy Family of Nazareth, founded in Poland. They staff (staffed?) several parish elementary schools in Philadelphia and nearby cities in the East. They own and operate Nazareth Academy, Holy Family College, and Nazareth Hospital in the Torresdale area of North Philadelphia.

I don't recall being nervous on the first day of school. The school was located just a block away from home. It was an easy walk that I must have done many times. On the first day of school, we were told to congregate in the parish hall to be assigned our teachers. I saw my friend Beerzy in the distance. I

called after him. "Beerzy, Beerzy, over here!"
Whack!!! Out of nowhere, I was slapped across the
face. "You don't holler when you are in school, young
man!" It was Sr. Simplicia, one of the three first grade
teachers. I immediately hoped that I would not get her
and luckily I did not because I soon found out (and
experienced) that she was tough. I had little or no
further experience with Sr. Simplicia while at St.
Adalbert's school, but I did run into her many years
later when, as a newly-ordained priest and teaching at
Father Judge High School in the Greater Northeast, I
was visiting a parent of a student at Nazareth Hospital.
I was in a crowded elevator when Sister entered the
elevator. I exclaimed, "Sr. Simplicia! How are you?
Do you remember me?" "No, Father, I don't," she
replied. In all innocence, with no intent to embarrass
her, I said, "You slapped me the first day of school at
St. Adalbert's years ago. Don't you remember?" "No,
Father, I don't," she repeated. The elevator door
opened; red faced and embarrassed, she quickly got

out. I don't think it was her floor to get out. I'm sure she punched eight and she got out at six.

I think I received a good education in grammar school. Some teachers were better than others. Some sisters, I thought, were too old to teach. Sr. Hugona, my fourth grade teacher, for example. She was old as dirt, as kids would say today. She confused my name with Dolores Orzechowka's name till the last day of school. It began to give me and Dolores identity crises.

Some grammar school incidents still stick out in my mind. I remember in the second grade I had a part in the school Christmas play. I was a black-faced page to one of the three kings. All I had to do was follow the king and hold his train. Still, this part made me so nervous that halfway through the performance, I peed my pants. I felt so sorry for the young Sister who afterwards had to unwind my soaked leggings.

Fr. Mike Szczygiel was our favorite assistant priest. He was a jovial, portly man, balding, in his forties, who looked and acted like Sidney Greenstreet, and who preached on Sundays in a high-pitched, singsongy voice. He smoked cigars, which was obvious when you went to him to confession, and he always wore a Homburg. He taught us religion once a month. We liked when he came because he was funny, he told jokes and stories, and he was a change from Sister.

It must have been one of the warmer months of our sixth grade year because the windows of our second-floor classroom were open. Father entered; we all dutifully stood up and said, *"Niech bedzie pochwalony Jesus Christus."* "May Jesus Christ be praised," a traditional Polish greeting, and Father responded, *"Na wieki wiekow. Amen,"* "Forever and ever. Amen." We sat down; Father placed his Homburg on Sister's desk and left the room to discuss with Sister what he was to teach, I suppose. Little mischievous Benny Szalejko, who sat in the front desk in front of Sister's desk because he was mischievous, leaned over, grabbed the Homburg and sailed it perfectly out the window on to the roof of the garages below our classroom. The boys laughed heartily; the girls giggled demurely. Father and Sister rushed in wondering what the commotion was about. Father noticed immediately his Homburg was gone. "Where is it?" he asked a few times, each time his voice getting louder and more high-pitched, just like in his sermons. Finally, one of the girls nodded in the direction of the window. Father looked out and saw his Homburg resting neatly on the roof of the garages housing the priests' cars. "Who did it? Who did it?" His voice became more high-pitched as he repeated the question several more times. And to the girls' credit, none of them told. It was a given that none of the boys would tell. Nobody wanted to be branded a "squealer." "All right! I'll beat it out of you!" he shouted. He took the heavy, thick pointer resting near the blackboard, grabbed Joey Andrzejewski sitting near the door, took him outside the door and beat his backside with the pointer. Joey came in teary-eyed. When it was soon my turn, after the first swat across the buttocks, which stung terribly, I placed my hands back behind me to ward off the next blow. The next few blows hurt as much as the first. When I reentered the classroom and sat down, I noticed the fingers of both hands all had huge blood blisters on them. But nobody squealed, and Fr. Mike was no longer our favorite priest because he couldn't take a joke, we thought.

59

As a seminarian I did keep in touch with Fr. Mike, as I called him, and when as a young priest teaching in Philadelphia I visited him in the hospital when I heard he was gravely ill with a severe case of diabetes. He confided in me that he would have left the priesthood years ago. "But what could I do if I did leave the priesthood?" he said. "Dig ditches? I couldn't do that." I found that honest statement shocking at the time because I was newly-ordained and had no intentions of leaving the priesthood. But now I believe that is the case of many priests. They remain in the priesthood for the security. I know the fear of the future deterred me from leaving the priesthood for several years. And I had some misgivings after leaving the priesthood especially when I was in Albany, New York, a few months after leaving, training to be a door-to-door insurance salesman for Combined Life Insurance Co., headquartered in Chicago. I roomed with a tough Puerto Rican, named Ramon, from New York City.

His Puerto Rican buddies would come into our room in the evening and talk and exchange lascivious jokes. I couldn't join in with them; I didn't know how if I wanted to. I remained in the corner of the room at my desk, trying to study, while they told dirty jokes, talked about their wives and girls back home, commented on our purported homosexual instructor, etc. They were really kind to me but they couldn't understand me. Why wouldn't I join in with them, they must have wondered. They felt sorry for me, as far as I could tell. They didn't realize I was going through a traumatic transition.

I recall going to Sunday Mass there in Albany. After Mass, I went to the rectory to speak to a priest. I was depressed and confused. I didn't want to be a door-to-door insurance salesman. I didn't believe in the product. I didn't believe in their tactics. They were trying to brainwash us. The elderly priest who answered the door was kind and understanding when I briefly told him of my situation. He invited me to stay awhile and have coffee while he had to go about doing his Sunday morning duties. I wished I could be doing them with him. Sunday mornings were the nicest part of the week for me as a priest. The atmosphere in the rectory brought back so many pleasant memories. I stayed for a few minutes and left for the hotel a few blocks away, wondering if I had made a mistake leaving the priesthood.

I recall, too, after I finished the training session and got my insurance license, selling insurance door-to-door in a poor neighborhood in North Tonawanda, New York, not far from where I once taught in Niagara Falls, New York, as a young priest. It was a bitter, cold, wintry day with freezing rain. After a few hours in the field without a single sale, second-guessing my decision to leave the priesthood, I knocked on a door. A little old lady looked at me. I began my usual spiel. She simply looked at me, not hearing a word I was saying. "Come in," she said. "You look cold. Icicles are forming in your hair and dripping from your eyelashes and your nose." (I hoped they were icicles dripping from my nose.) I didn't sell her any insurance, but I did thaw out, for which I was grateful to her, and continued on past Our Lady of Czestochowa Church, a Polish church where I said Mass and heard confessions on occasion when I was teaching at Bishop Duffy High School. What I wouldn't have given for the warm security of that rectory on that cold blustery day. I felt like the prodigal son in Jesus' parable. Maybe I should go back to the safety and security of my Father's home, the priesthood.

I almost lost my job with Combined Life Insurance at our first regional meeting at a Holiday Inn in Canandaigua, NY. After all day of listening to numerous pep talks by various managers and district supervisors, we were told to assemble in the grand ballroom for the closing ceremony where we were to pledge our allegiance, our loyalty, our fealty, to the regional supervisor. From his elevated chair (throne?), he cajoled us, he urged us, he threatened us, he promised us riches and rewards if we promised him our loyalty. He sat down and we were to come up to him individually, kneel before him and place our folded hands into his hands that he would cup over our hands as we promised him our loyalty and dedication. This was too much for me. I didn't mind going through this ritual at my ordination to the priesthood before the bishop but not before a regional supervisor of a very suspect insurance company working on its employees' lower emotions of fear and greed. I told my local manager, Pete, a Catholic from Niagara Falls, who knew I was a former priest, that I refused to participate in this ritual. I said, "This borders on the sacrilegious, Pete. I can't do it." He urged me: "If you don't, you're fired, Ed. Everybody has to go through with this." To my shame, I went through with it. That's how desperate I was for a job because at that point I was destitute. I left the priesthood with $400, which was soon spent.

60

St. Adalbert's was a big parish with a big grammar school. We had eight grades with three classes to a grade and about 30 students, boys and girls, to a class. All the teachers were nuns who lived in a convent next to the school across the street from Mr. Gniewek's bar, which was directly across from the chapel. We were taught religion in Polish, and we had a class in the Polish language, which was really unnecessary because practically all of us spoke Polish. My favorite period was a 15-minute recess at 10:30 in the morning. It seemed as if everyday, while running around, I would bump into somebody and have the wind knocked out of me. That was a terrible feeling, waiting for the wind to inflate my lungs again, thinking I was going to die if that air didn't come soon. Or if I didn't have the wind knocked out of me, I would bump heads with somebody, leaving me with a metallic ringing sensation in my head, ears and mouth.

The outdoor dungeon-like toilets in the school yard were depressing and forbidding. We walked down about 15 steep steps to face about ten urinals and five stalls. Often, to liven things up a little, we would see who could urinate the highest on the wall above the urinals. And so how coincidental and how it brought back memories when many years later, Fr. Bill Lyman, a classmate of mine (Who also left the priesthood, has a family and is a marriage counselor in New Jersey), told me the following joke during an annual retreat we made together at the Oblate Retreat House in Allentown, PA. "Sister went over to the rectory. 'Father, the boys are acting up in the lavatory. I don't know how to say this delicately, but they are competing as to who can urinate the highest on the wall.' Father said, 'Okay, Sister, I'll take care of it.' A few minutes later Sister saw Father and asked, 'What did you do when you found the boys urinating on the wall, Father?' 'I hit the ceiling,' he responded." I remember Bill told me another joke that I think is worth repeating. I at least remembered it all these years. "The mother of Elvis Presley was going to sue the reporter who tagged Elvis Presley with the nickname 'Elvis the Pelvis.'" Taking the hook, I asked, "Why?" "She had another son whose name was Enos."

I rarely if ever missed school. If I was sick with a fever, Mom would send me to Sitko's Pharmacy around the corner on Allegheny Avenue to get some castor oil. For a quarter Mr. Sitko would give me about six ounces of castor oil. I think I was supposed to drink a spoonful and I suggested that to my mother, but she felt more was better. I would stand on a chair over the kitchen sink, in case I regurgitated, which was quite likely, holding my nose with one hand, with the other hand I would drink down as quickly as I could the castor oil. Each time I took castor oil this way, it became more difficult to do so and I came closer to regurgitating. The taste and smell and texture of the oil were so awful. Finally, it got to the point I refused. I said I couldn't drink the castor oil. Mom then got the idea of putting the oil in orange juice. That helped considerably. But after a while I couldn't drink castor oil even with orange juice and I couldn't drink or smell orange juice alone without the possibility of regurgitating until well into my seminary days.

I do remember missing one day of grammar school. It happened in the eighth grade near graduation. Gypsy Rose Lee and her sister Sally Rand were the rage of strip-tease burlesque queens back then. Sally Rand, along with her long, white decorative fans, was coming next week to the Trocadero (the "Troc" for short) at Eighth and Arch Streets in downtown Philadelphia. Beerzy and I plotted how to catch her matinee the following Wednesday. We saved up our money and instead of going to school that day, we took a detour to the park. We placed our copy books under a bench and lightly covered them with some dirt and hopped the 60 trolley to K&A to catch the El to downtown Philly to Eighth Street. With trepidation, we went to the admissions box, wondering whether we would get in or not. Beerzy and I were both tall for our age and could possibly pass for 16. Was that the admissions age? We didn't know, but they took our money and allowed us in. We were so nervous, so afraid, so guilt-ridden that we didn't enjoy the show and regretted ever coming there. We quickly left the place and headed back home to the park only to find our notebooks gone—a further sign that we should have never gone there in the first place. Now I really had something to confess that Saturday, I thought.

As eighth graders, our final year, we became bolder I suppose. On our way home for lunch, several of us decided to climb the inside of one of the two tall steeples of the church, the steeple that functioned as a bell tower as well. We were always curious to see what was up there and what kind of view there was from the top of the steeple. We slowly walked up the narrow, circular, dusty stairs, frequently pushing aside spider webs and cobwebs along the way. It seemed these steps weren't trodden for years, possibly for decades. We looked up and saw we had about another thirty feet to go. With trepidation we proceeded, wondering whether it was such a good idea to climb these steep steeple stairs to begin with. We were trespassing on a part of the church. We finally couldn't go any higher. We came upon a huge bell encircled by a catwalk. We felt triumphant. We probably did something no other St. Adalbert student ever did. We must have experienced the same exhilaration that the first conquerors of Mt. Everest did. We examined the bell carefully; we touched it reverently as if it were the Liberty Bell. We then turned our attention outward to the small peepholes that gave us a panoramic view of Allegheny Avenue. We saw the roofs of all the buildings beneath us; we were above the tallest trees of the park. The people and cars along Allegheny Avenue seemed slightly smaller. And as we were about to turn to leave, the bell began to move slowly. We were petrified. We watched as the bell reached its apogee until it almost overturned and then emitted a tremendous sound that we thought would burst our eardrums. Filled with fright, panicking, we stumbled over one another tying to be the first one down the steps. We reached the bottom of the steps, flung open the door only to find the non-phased sexton, Mr. Fronczak, pulling mightily on the bell rope announcing to the entire neighborhood that it was time to pray the noonday Angelus Prayer.

After celebration of Mass at St. Adalbert's Church. 1971.

61

There certainly is no skyline of Port Richmond to speak of. The tallest building, probably, is the grain elevator on the banks of the Delaware River, where grain, delivered by freighters from all over the world, was stored and then delivered by train throughout the area. But the twin steeples of our gothic St. Adalbert's church that can be seen from miles away on the nearby I-95 highway came a close second in height to the mighty grain elevator. It is a tall, majestic church, especially for a simple parish church, made out of gray stone with small, hardly noticeable buttresses to support the external steep, copper lined roof and the high internal ribbed vaulted ceiling, exemplified by many of the great European cathedrals of the Middle Ages. A half dozen marble steps led to each of three tall pointed entrance doors. The vestibule is small. The nave or the central part of the church from the vestibule to the sanctuary is long and narrow, leading to an impressive high wooden gold plated main altar, ornately decorated with statues of St. Peter and St. Paul and a painting of Our Lady's Assumption between them and a large crucifix above the painting. On special feasts this painting of Our Lady's Assumption into Heaven was lowered to reveal a sculpture of the Blessed Mother holding the Baby Jesus. As a child I was intrigued by this lowering of the painting and the revelation of the sculpture behind it. It was magical; it was miraculous to my young mind.

In the center slightly above the altar where Mass was celebrated was the tabernacle, the Holy of Holies, where the Blessed Sacrament for Holy Communion was kept and where the Sacred Host for adoration was reserved. The priest would get the large golden key at the side of the tabernacle, genuflect, open the thick, golden outer door of the tabernacle, then genuflect again and open a thinner golden inner door, reach in for the Blessed Sacrament and again genuflect before turning to the congregation, to invite them to receive Holy Communion. I was always fascinated by this ritual as a youngster, wondering what else was in that tabernacle besides the ciboria filled with Sacred Hosts, not realizing that years later I would often enter into that Holy of Holies and go through that ritual myself.

Originally, there were two marble statues of angels, one on either side of the altar on the floor of the sanctuary, holding lamps in their hands that provided most of the light in the sanctuary. The angels were removed some years ago probably, even though they were angels without corporeal bodies, for taking up too much space in the sanctuary or for being too garish. Contrary to present-day official church instructions, St. Adalberts still has the altar rail, still separating the congregation from what is taking place at the altar of sacrifice. The tabernacle is still where it's always been—behind the main altar. The pulpit was located amongst the pews near the front left corner of the church. The priest preached from the pulpit at Sunday's 12 o'clock Solemn High Mass and on special feasts. It was removed years ago because it obstructed the view of the altar to many of the worshippers on that side of the church.

There are 8 columns, four on each side of the church near the side aisles, supporting the high vaulted ceiling. The twelve tall, pointed, stained glass windows, six on either wall, were of prominent Polish saints and of scenes from the bible, much after the manner of medieval cathedrals before the invention of the printing press. I remember preaching about them one Sunday morning when I was home for vacation because I felt very few of the parishioners ever adverted to these stained glass windows and their messages.

I estimate the church can seat a 1,000 people and stand another 300. Almost every Sunday Mass, when I was a child, it was filled to capacity, often with standing room only. I went to the 10:30 Mass a few years ago and felt sorry for the frustrated pastor, who was the celebrant. He preached to about a 100 people scattered throughout the church, berating them for not coming to church (when they were actually there), comparing present day church attendance to how it was years ago, in our day, when the church was packed at all the Sunday masses. He said the parish could not continue to survive if more people did not come to church and did not donate more money. I read a recent St. Adalbert's parish bulletin, printed in English and Polish, stating their weekly collection amounted to $4,500. The small Italian parish we belong to here in Lockport, St. Joseph's, collects that amount. I suspect many of the present St. Adalbert's parishioners are recent immigrants from Poland, and not so generous and loyal to the church as our parents were because of their long subjugation under Communist rule.

The other two buildings dotting the "Port Richmond skyline" are the other two churches on Allegheny Avenue almost directly across from each other: The Nativity of the Blessed Virgin Mary church, the Irish church, and Our Lady Help of Christians, the German church. The Nativity (I'm not sure how many Port Richmondites know what "nativity" means and if they do, I'm not sure they know it is the nativity of Mary. Everybody refers to the church as simply "the Nativity.") It is more massive, bigger than St.

Adalbert's church, but not quite as tall and of a totally different architectural style. My guess is it is either the Norman or Romanesque style, both characterized by heavy masonry and the use of the round arch and the vaulted roof. Although I said Mass there a few times, I spent most of my time praying in their cool basement church, which was open all day long, when I was home on vacation.

Our Lady Help of Christians is definitely Gothic, almost identical to St. Adalberts Church, except on a smaller scale and with one steeple. One thing many Richmondites were and are still grateful to Our Lady Help of Christians church is the clock at the top of the steeple. Many of us during our childhood kept track of time during the day by that clock that chimed every hour.

62

Sr. Fides, my eighth-grade teacher, was my favorite teacher, which is usually the case with eighth-grade teachers, I suppose. She was relatively young, in her late twenties, of medium height and stature, with a beautiful face, a slightly pointed noise, and a pleasant disposition. She never raised her voice, never struck anybody, and she seemed especially pious, even for nuns. She had the habit of pulling her veil up and over her right shoulder as she taught. She was the first one to give me the idea of becoming a priest by just dropping a hint here and a hint there. A few years after I graduated she was transferred, and I lost contact with her until very recently. Probably in her early eighties, she now lives in Connecticut in the congregation's retirement home. I wrote her a letter and tried to refresh her memory of who I was by telling her a few things about myself and that I became a priest and left the priesthood and got married. I asked her about herself and invited her to start up a correspondence.

"I'll tell you what I have done with my life since grammar school, Sister, and I would like to know what you have done," I wrote. She wrote me a brief note saying she will pray for me and she sent me a holy card. I think Sister believes I'm going to hell and doesn't want to associate with me. I hope she's wrong.

I think I was always afraid (and still am slightly in my more irrational moments) of going to hell, probably because of the fire and brimstone sermons preached in my youth and the sermonettes and lectures of the nuns and more probably because of the grotesque picture that hung above my bed all during my childhood. It was a large picture with a tarnished gold emblazoned frame. At the top of the picture, was an angry gray-headed and gray-bearded God the Father, scowling at numerous suffering people, looking plaintively at Him. These souls with anguished faces and imploring hands were prevented from getting out of the pit by black, naked, muscular bodies with horns on their heads and pitchforks in their hands, goading them back into the pit.

Ed Chrzanowski

Imagine, this was the final picture I went to bed with all during my childhood. No wonder I still fear hell and it's a wonder I didn't have nightmares every night.

To allay my fears of hell, I remind myself of a saying of St. Francis de Sales, a saint and a Doctor of the Church, which means, according to the church, whatever he said or wrote must be true. He wrote: "I would rather be judged by God than by own sweet mother." That's what I'm relying on, God's infinite loving mercy. I am also consoled by a teaching of a prominent modern theologian that *after* death, when we will be freed of the distractions of this flesh and this world—when such an important decision deserves such clarity and freedom—we will be given the opportunity of deciding if we wish to spend eternity with God or spend eternity separated from Him. No longer am I afraid of dying suddenly, accidentally, of having a safe drop on my head or being hit by a car. When I die, *after I die*, I plan on opting to spend eternity with God.

63

About one-third of the boys graduating from the eighth grade went to Northeast Catholic High School, located a block from the Erie-Torresdale El station, two stops north, or about five minutes from the Allegheny Station. When I entered Northeast Catholic in 1943, with almost 4,000 students, it was considered the largest Catholic high school for boys in the world. It was and still is staffed by the Oblates of St. Francis de Sales, a congregation of priests and brothers founded in France in the late 19th century. The mission of the congregation is to perpetuate the spirit and teachings of St. Francis de Sales, who died in the early 17th century in the eastern part of France in the charming city of Annecy near Geneva, Switzerland. My wife and I visited there several years ago. I saw the vestments he wore; I saw the cathedral where he said Mass and preached; I saw the manuscripts of his books and letters. I put my fingers in the same holy water font that he did every morning; I opened the same door he opened as he entered the chapel to say Mass for his beloved Visitandine Sisters that he and St. Jane de Chantel founded in Annecy.

Francis is known as the "Gentleman Saint." He emphasized gentleness. "Be gentle with yourself first and then with your neighbor," he wrote. I liked St. Francis de Sales's spirit and I hope some of it has infused me. In the main, the priest/teachers were gentle but sometimes they resorted to rough measures, as when Fr. Larry Knebels, a nice, gentle math teacher ordinarily, beat up a poor freshman for turning on and off the classroom light switch. Or when rough-looking, tough-sounding Fr. Nick DiEnno literally punched in the face a half-dozen seniors who were acting up in a crowded corridor during a mock air-raid drill.

In the eighth grade we all took an IQ test and we were placed in the freshman class at the high school according to the results. With my IQ score of 118 (I looked it up later when I taught at North Catholic as a seminarian), I was placed in Section 3. Not bad considering there were more than 20 sections our freshman year and not bad considering that English could practically be considered my second language since my parents spoke no English at home. But I did read quite a bit during my grammar school days, which, I believe, helped a lot. I remember going to the public library at Almond and Ann Streets, sometimes to fool around, and sometimes to pick up a book from the "Hardy Boys' Series" to books by Rafael Sabatini that are still popular today. I recently went to our local library here in Lockport to check up on "The Tom Swift Series" that I enjoyed very much as a child. I asked the elderly librarian if he heard of the series. He mused a moment and said, "Yes, I do. But they were around during my parents' time." He made me feel older than I am. He checked his computer and said, "Yes, here they are. But they are not in general circulation. They are now collectibles. They were first published in 1912."

The first four sections took college preparatory courses. English, math, history, French, religion, Latin and an elective. I didn't do anything auspicious during my four years of high school, except make the varsity bowling team all four years and occasionally made the honor roll and received an honorable mention at graduation for the Scholar/Athlete Award, probably as a reward for my going into the Oblates. I wanted to try out for other sports, but I was too shy. At that age, I was even too shy to try out for sandlot football in the neighborhood, but I was forced into it.

64

There were two football teams in the neighborhood: the Venango Cubs, for kids under 16 and the Venango Bears for kids over 16. One Sunday we went to watch the Cubs play at their field at Venango and Richmond Streets. Before the game the coach asked us bystanders if any of us wanted to play that day. They were short a player. "Go ahead, Wimp. You're always telling us how you'd like to try football. Here's your chance," said Sajo. The coach put together a uniform. I went behind the bushes, changed and came out for the opening kickoff. I was placed at right guard on offense and defense. On offense, I was told to block my opponent to the right if the ball carrier was going to the left and to the left if the ball carrier was going to the right. On defense, I was told nothing. I didn't know that I was supposed to try to penetrate the line and tackle the ball carrier. The coaches must have presumed I knew that. I got into the defensive stance when the opposing team had the ball, but instead of rushing forward I backed off a few yards into what would now be known as the middle-linebacker position. I went unblocked the whole game and I made a slew of tackles, dozens of them. In fact, I was the defensive hero of the game. Immediately, I became a neighborhood sensation. It seemed as if every kid in the neighborhood was congratulating me for the great game I played. In fact, our coach at Northeast Catholic High School, Johnny Gillespie, heard of me and had me scouted. The next week he came to our classroom and in front of the class he tried to recruit me. "Wouldn't you rather play for your school than for your neighborhood?" he argued. That afternoon he had me out on the practice field in full uniform and had his running backs run at me one at a time for about an hour, and I had to try to tackle them. That's what my tryout consisted of. I don't even know whether I made the team or not. But it didn't matter. I never went back, and I did prefer to play with people I knew and for people who knew me.

The following year, under the sponsorship of the Polish American Club, we started our own team, entered it into the Pop Warner Conference, a citywide sandlot league, and proudly called ourselves the Richmond Redskins. The club gave us a room to dress in. When we played at home, we had to prepare the field which was right across the Polish American Club on Allegheny Avenue. I was probably the youngest player on the team and one of the smaller linemen. I played tackle behind Reds Haber, but I played offense ahead of Reds only because Reds would not practice and did not know the offensive plays.

Actually, we had a very good team. Most of the players were grown men. Some were former high school standouts; a few were college players. One player, our fullback Frank Stanczak, made Little All-American at Lafayette College the year before. We drew several thousand fans at home games and several busloads of fans to away games, primarily because of Beebo. He was a great halfback who could run, pass and punt the ball, if his older brother Gene wasn't available for punting. Even Googoo was not a bad wide receiver.

Our equipment was similar to today's except for the helmet. It was made of soft leather and had no face guard, which is what made me quit playing football after the first year. During an inter-squad scrimmage, I was involved in a late tackle, flying through the air, when the ball carrier, an older, wily player, a married man named Alex, already down on the ground, raised his knee right into my face. I ended up with a broken nose and a deviated septum that prevented me from breathing properly for years until I had the deviated septum corrected while in the seminary. What discouraged me from playing the following year was the attitude the team took towards my injury. At a team meeting they narrowly passed in a vote to reimburse me the doctor's expenses for resetting my nose. Suppose I was hurt again, more seriously? Suppose it was me, instead of Frank Stanczak, who, on the opening kickoff, tackled (more like collided with) the big fullback when both were running at full speed and who sent the fullback to the hospital with broken ribs? Maybe I would have gotten the broken ribs. I took pride in my courage, in my guts, when it came to tackling. Those who didn't have guts, I thought, tackled high around the shoulders or around the head. But those who had guts, braving a knee or shoe in the face, tackled at the knees if not lower, when necessary. That's how I tackled because I had guts, I figured.

But this one play still terrifies me to this day. It's etched in my memory, and I relive it when I see kickoff returns on television. And if the truth be known, I slowed down, I chickened out, I allowed Frank Stanczak to get ahead of me, to get to that fullback first because I was scared stiff; my guts failed me. With every stride I was telling myself, "It's their fullback who is supposed to be so tough has the ball, and he's running right at me. I'm running right at him. What should I do? This collision is going to take place in full view of everybody unless I slow down, unless I trip. He's outrunning his blockers and, surprisingly, I'm outrunning everybody on our team. Where are my teammates? Are they deliberately slowing down because they're scared too? It's going to be an open-field tackle if it happens. I can't fake that I missed the tackle. Should I stumble and fall? That would be too obvious. I know. I'll slow down and maybe somebody will beat me to him." I thought all that in the 5 or 10 seconds that kickoff play was developing. And that's what happened. I slowed down and, thank God, Frank Stanczak, our All-American fullback from Lafayette College, collided with their big fullback and sent him to the hospital. I don't think the viewing public of professional football realizes the courage it takes to be what they now call a special-teams player.

I recall another game against an Italian team from South Philly, the Tasker Bears. I guess I accidentally on purpose clipped one of their players and forced him out of the game with a sprained knee. Clipping was and is illegal. It means you block a defender below the waist from behind. Now, it's blocking him anywhere in the back. The remainder of the game my opponent across the line, who looked about 40 years old with a heavy beard and looked about 250 pounds, was cursing me and threatening to get even with me for my dirty play. I wanted to apologize to him, tell him I didn't mean it. I was sorry. But under the circumstances, I didn't think an apology was fitting. Here I was 16-years old, a beginning shaver, weighing about 200 pounds being intimidated and cursed at by a 250 40-year old bearded monster and who now will have to go to confession because I heard all those curse words directed at me. Except for throwing an elbow at me here and there, he never did get to me.

I also recall our bread-and-butter play, good for three or four yards every time. In the huddle the quarterback would say: "T-5 on three." That meant it was off my left tackle position or hole 5 at the count of three. The end and I cross-blocked. He would block my tackle in, I would block his end out and the center would pull out and block the linebacker. Almost every time we needed three or four yards for a first down or touchdown, we called that play, and almost every time it was successful.

I did not go out for the Richmond Redskins Football Team the following year, for fear of getting hurt, for fear of what my father would say or do if he had to pay a hefty medical bill, but I did follow the team. I took the bus along with a bunch of guys and girls from the neighborhood to watch the Richmond Redskins play the Gratersford State Penitentiary football team. I recall having to go through a metal detector, just like the movies. I recall the inmates in the stands to the right of us, ogling the girls, making off-color remarks. I recall one of their players getting hurt and being carried off on a stretcher and one of the inmates in the stands hollering, "That's okay. He's got plenty of time to get better. He's in here for life."

Our team did not get paid for this game, just a free dinner for the team and its fans. I found it fascinating to be waited on by real-live convicts, not realizing that years later after I left the priesthood I would hobnob with hardened criminals on a daily basis for eight years when I taught English and philosophy and was a full-time counselor in a college program at Attica State Prison here in western New York.

Ed Chrzanowski

65

I began my nine-year Attica career a few years after leaving the priesthood. I found those years eventful, interesting, educational, eye-opening. The stereotypes of viewing prison life were removed and I am grateful for the experience.

A Fr. Tom McHugh, an Oblate of St. Francis De Sales priest, ordained a year ahead of me, was assistant director of the program. He got me the job. After two years of teaching part-time at Attica State Prison in a college program, teaching part-time at Albion Correctional Facility, teaching part-time at Niagara County Community College, and writing part-time for the local paper, the *Buffalo News,* all at the same time, I was asked to work full-time at Attica as a counselor in a college program.

My job was to supervise 40 college student-inmates involved in a tutorial program. These 40 inmates were housed together on the same company, 30 Company, C Block. Their facility job was to tutor and be tutored by other inmates, for which they received twelve cents an hour. The tutoring took place twice a day, three hours in the morning and three hours in the afternoon in a large barred room called the Day Room for 30 Company. In the evenings these inmates involved in this tutorial program, along with about 100 other students housed throughout the prison and involved in other facility jobs, attended 3-hour classes 5 days a week in the school, located in D Block on the other side of the prison. My job was to see that the inmates assigned to the program attended these tutorial sessions, that they studied, they tutored or were tutored, and they behaved themselves. The Day Room was all concrete and steel and some wood. Every little sound carried. The Day Room was equipped with chairs, desks, study carrels, a small library, a supply cabinet, typewriters, and a computer. And I was locked in with these 40 inmates six hours a day. A guard's station that controlled the cell doors of the entire Company was right outside the Day Room. If trouble developed, the guard would summon help, which, on few occasions he had to do. In addition, one evening a week, I taught an English class one semester and a philosophy class the next.

During these tutorial sessions I answered questions, tutored, helped with papers, and, most of the time, counseled by just listening to the inmates' problems and concerns and offering advice. Early on the job, a white inmate from Buffalo named John, a Vietnam veteran who after his discharge went on a drug-driven spree and killed a few people and was now serving life, said, "You know, Ed, looking around this Day Room, I'd say that 90% of these guys have bodies." I knew what he meant and I doubted it. But as time went on and more inmates confided in me, I'd have to say that his estimate was correct: about 90% of these inmates were in prison for killing someone.

There were some funny and not-so funny incidents that took place in and out of that Day Room during those years. I recall during a Day Room session a commotion took place in an adjoining Day Room where haircuts were given and where medication was dispensed. A full-length barred door was between the two Day Rooms. We heard a commotion in the other Day Room; chairs and tables were being overturned. "Fight! Fight!" somebody in our Day Room hollered. We all rushed to the barred door and saw a petite white nurse in a white nurse's uniform chasing a 6'4" black inmate around the Day Room, and he was overturning chairs to obstruct her path. "So you like white meat, do you? I'll give you something white!" as she was chasing him and trying to squirt him with a cold cream squeeze dispenser.

I saw the nurse the next day in the Officers' Cafeteria. She smiled. She said she had to keep her sense of humor if she wanted to survive in her job.

I had been trying for months to enroll Kevin, a homeboy (from Lockport) inmate into our college tutorial program but with no success. One day outside our Day Room window was Kevin hanging on the window bars, hollering, "Let me in! Let me in! I want to come in!" The irony, of course, was everybody wanted to get out. Kevin was washing the outside windows and was only joking. He never joined the college program. He has since been released, and I've spoken with him several times in a local supermarket. He appeared to be doing well. But his brother told me recently that Kevin is back in Attica on a drug charge.

Bobby, a tall middle-age, Black inmate, a conscientious student, asked permission to take one of the manual typewriters from the Day Room to his cell to finish a paper. I gave him permission. Two days later when I arrived at the Day Room, I found out that Bobby was involved in a fight with shanks (inmate-made daggers) with another inmate in the mess hall. It seemed the two men had pre-arranged the time and place of the fight. Both were badly lacerated before guards stopped the fight. One woman guard in defense of another guard, was also badly lacerated. Several of our student-inmates told me they were in a position to rescue the woman-guard and felt bad for not doing so, but it was against a prison code to defend a guard, man or woman, against an inmate. "She knew what she was getting into," one inmate told me. When I retrieved the typewriter from Bobby's cell that day, I noticed the thin piece of metal that held the paper down and in place was missing. Apparently, Bobby shaved it into a point, attached it to a wooden handle, covered it with tape and used it as a shank, a homemade dagger. I never told the prison authorities where Bobby got the makings of that shank. It would only get us into trouble.

I did this work for nine years, not realizing how much tension I was under, how my nerves were slowly being frayed, how indifferent, insensitive I was becoming to the plight of the inmates, whose cause I championed when I first began the job. My indifference, my insensitivity struck me one evening when, as I was on my way out to go home, all the gates were suddenly locked down because there was a stabbing in the C-Block yard. This meant a delay of about half-an-hour. Annoyed, I dropped my book bag to the ground, leaned against the corridor wall and looked casually at my watch. And I looked just as casually a few minutes later at the bloodied body of an inmate being wheeled in from the yard to the infirmary on a gurney. He had one arm hanging over the gurney, dripping blood. I hardly looked at the inmate; the blood didn't phase me. It was as if this were commonplace. (Stabbings did happen frequently enough.) "Why couldn't this have happened ten minutes later," I thought. "I would have been out of here," almost blaming the possibly dying inmate for my delay. As I drove home that night, this incident and my reaction to it made me think: "Maybe I've been here too long. Maybe it's time to get out, if I react this way to a stabbing."

I enjoyed my work at Attica in a sort of masochistic way. I found the work rewarding; most of the inmates appreciated what we were trying to do for them. Their response and enthusiasm in the classroom was far better than I and other teachers ever received out "on the streets." I felt my work with the inmates was an extension of my former priestly ministry and I was saddened when it suddenly came to a crashing halt.

Martin, a burly black man in his early 40s, a recent transfer from A Block, the psychiatric block, to 30 Company, C Block, and our tutorial program, was acting strangely one morning in the Day Room. The other inmates shied away from him for fear that he might "go off." He was walking around the Day Room hurriedly and nervously, smoking, stopping every once in a while and talking to an imaginary person. I knew Martin. I had him for class the previous semester; he was a good and conscientious English student who seemed very happy to get out of A Block into C Block and the college program. I called him over to my desk. He had difficulty sitting still, difficulty concentrating. He said he was depressed. He realized he would never see the streets again. And as the cigarette between his fingers was getting smaller until it burnt his fingers and he had to throw it away, he said he missed women. He said he was married but that his wife divorced him two years ago. I noticed he was searching his pockets for something.

"What are you looking for, Marty?" I asked.

"Cigarettes. I'm out of cigarettes."

"When is your commissary day?"

"In three days."

"What do you smoke?"

"Kools."

The bell rang. The barred door slid open. I immediately called his prison counselor. He told me to call the prison psychiatrist. I called the prison psychiatrist. He told me to see that Martin continued taking his medication.

On my way to work the next morning, I bought the morning edition of the *Buffalo News,* three packs of Kools and placed them in my book-bag. The guards never checked my bag and I never had to go through the metal detector. But this day, which happened about once every three months, everybody, including lawyers, judges, guards, even the warden, the chaplain, had to go through the metal detector and had the contents of their bags searched as they entered the facility. The guard opened my book-bag, took the newspaper as contraband, said nothing about the cigarettes and allowed me through.

That morning before the study session, I went to Martin's cell and handed him the 3 packs of Kools through the 6" by 8" opening in his cell door. He thanked me profusely. He said he was not coming to the Day Room that day. He was not feeling well. I asked if he was taking his medication. He said he would.

That evening I taught my evening class and stayed a little longer to catch up on some work. I closed up the school. As I was leaving, the guard at the final door (There are 12 locked doors you must go through before you leave the facility.) asked me my name. He told me to wait. He got on the phone and said, "We got your man, captain." The captain in a freshly ironed white shirt soon arrived.

"Open your bag. Where are the cigarettes? What did you do with them?"

"I gave them to an inmate who was having psychiatric problems."

"Okay, you can go."

The following morning, my civilian superior, Bob Hausrath, came to the Day Room, which he rarely did. I knew something was up. "Get all your stuff together. The warden wants you out of the prison immediately." That same day, I met with Bob at his office in Buffalo. He asked if I smuggled anything else, any drugs, into the facility. He said the prison authorities suspected me of bringing in drugs because a lot of drugs were getting into the facility lately. I, of course, said no. But the banishment stood. I was no longer able to work or teach in any state prison.

66

Nor did Lenny, our starting center, both ways—offense and defense, for the Richmond Redskins, realize, nor did any of us at the time realize, that while he was playing against the Gratersford State Prison Football Team that in a few short years he would be playing center, both ways, for the Gratersford State Prison Football Team. The police caught Lenny, in the middle of the night, carrying a case of liquor on his back from the backdoor of the Polish American Club. He was sentenced two to five years and ended up in Gratersford State Prison, about 30 miles west of Phildelphia.

While teaching at Northeast Catholic High School as a seminarian, I romanticized: "Gee, here are two childhood buddies from the same rough neighborhood: one studying for the priesthood, the other in prison for a felony. Just like in the Spencer Tracy-James Cagney movies. "It's better than the 'Dead End Kids,'" as Beerzy would say. I went out to visit Lenny. We had a pleasant visit. He said he was doing well and hoped to get out on parole shortly, which he did. After his release, Lenny never got into trouble with the law again. I guess he learned his lesson or maybe he just never got caught again.

67

In my junior year at Northeast Catholic, I befriended four classmates in my section, Junior One, which meant we were taking third year Latin. John Murphy was a tall, lanky kid. He was a whiz at math, a great golfer. Unfortunately, we did not have golf as a sport in high school then because John would certainly have made the team. He was built like and could hit a ball almost as long as Tiger Woods, but not as accurate. He introduced me to the game in high school and we played at least once every summer after our ordination to the priesthood. John also joined the Oblates. As a priest he wanted to pursue a pro career in golf but was denied permission by his superiors.

John was a severe diabetic. In the seminary we often played basketball against each other. We often played on opposing teams and guarded each other. John was slightly taller than I and out-rebounded me and outscored me. I would be patient for the first half-hour or so when his insulin would begin to wear off, and he became sluggish and lost his agility. Then I took over the boards and then I began to outscore him. It was not very Christian for me to do that, I know, but I had no other choice.

While golfing one day in Philadelphia after we were ordained, out on the 9th hole of an exclusive country club, the furthest hole from the clubhouse, John was slowly going into insulin shock. He looked into his golf bag for the ever-present bar of chocolate. There was none. He forgot. We started walking to the clubhouse, but John couldn't walk any further. His muscles became spasmodic. He attempted with my assistance to scale the fence that encircled the course. He couldn't make it. He lost all control of his limbs. He then slumped against a tree, still shaking spasmodically, about to fall into a coma. I ran the ½ mile or so to the clubhouse. I asked for a doctor. Luckily, there was one who just finished his round of golf. He poured lots of sugar into a container of orange juice provided by the bartender. We both hopped into a golf cart and found John barely conscious. The doctor poured the juice into John's mouth. After about five minutes, John got up and we finished the round. Thanks, Doc, where ever you are. And thanks, John, for being such a good friend, and I know where you are. John died about a year ago in North Carolina where he was pastor for about twenty years. He died of complications from a car accident that resulted from passing out while behind the wheel.

Gene Boyle was a good-looking, heavy-bearded Irishman even in high school. He was bright, and he was a hustler. He was always finding ways to make money. At Christmas time he made lots of money selling shopping bags in downtown Philadelphia, and he knew how to hold on to the money. Almost every day he mooched his lunch from the rest of us. After graduation I lost contact with him. After I left the priesthood, I got reconnected with him. He took my wife and me, when we were visiting my brother Joe and his wife Jean, to lunch one day at a fancy restaurant in Bristol, slightly north of Philadelphia and told us his life story, which was not pleasant. He had built up a very successful private investigative agency, and he was in the midst of a nasty divorce settlement. His wife wanted half the business. He refused. He was adamant. "I don't care if they throw me in jail. She is not getting half of my business." He hadn't changed much from his high school days. He still wanted to hold on to what he had. He said he was suffering from high blood pressure over the divorce settlement. The judge was about to threaten him with imprisonment if he did not comply with his order. He took us that evening to his favorite social club near North Catholic. It seemed that Gene had forgotten his marital woes that night as he danced with every unattached girl in the place. And, surprisingly, he said he became fast friends with Beebo who frequented that club but was not there that particular evening. I read in our alumni newspaper that Gene died a few years later. I never heard about the resolution of his divorce settlement; I don't know if he ever went to jail. But I do think his divorce woes contributed mightily to his death.

John Collins was always neatly dressed, well-organized, bright, disciplined and I always suspected came from a wealthy family. He took a train to school every day from a rich suburb north of Philadelphia, Yardley. John knew how to make the best use of his time, apparently. He consistently made the honor roll while carrying a heavy academic schedule. He spent at least two hours a day traveling to and from school and he still managed to gain a pilot's license at the young age of 16. John belonged to the Flying Falcons Club, moderated by Fr. Harry Minnick, an airplane buff. During and after school, students learned the intricacies of the workings of an actual plane in the basement of the faculty house next to the school, took aeronautical classes and eventually flew and got their pilots' licenses.

After graduation from Johns Hopkins University where he gained his law degree and almost lost his faith, John moved to Spain in quest of peace of mind and his faith again. The next thing I heard he was living outside Philadelphia in Yardley again, was married, had a family and a successful law practice. After almost 40 years, John and I got reconnected through a cousin of mine whose divorce case John handled, much more amicably, I presume, than Gene's. Shirley and I met John, his wife, Kathy, and two daughters when they stopped in Niagara Falls, Ontario, Canada, on their way to Toronto to see their son who was studying drama there. We also visited John and his wife at their plush home in Yardley. John has sold his practice and is now happily semi-retired, doing "pro bono" work for the diocese, philosophizing, writing "daily miscellanies," short, pithy philosophical observations. Here are a few samples of some of his latest that he gave me on a recent visit to his home:

A PROGRAM FOR LIFE: In youth, Experience; in middle age, Reflection; in old age, Contemplation!

SUCCESS IS LIKE SEX, it promises a heightened sense of being!

WE WILL TO KNOW what is necessary to our well-being!

WE MUST LEARN TO LIVE with energies of our being in tandem!

THINKING WITHOUT JUDGING is like running without stopping!

THE FORM or STRUCTURE OF THE KNOWER is as important a factor in knowing as the form or structure of the known!

RECOGNITION REQUIRES prior cognition!

A FIELD OF FLOWERS doesn't bloom all at once and altogether, and neither does the kingdom of God!

THERE ARE THOSE WHO SIMMER in life, and those who come to a boil!

IT'S HARD TO LOVE YOUR NEIGHBOR if you don't love your self!

GOD IMPULSES, PROMPTS and INSPIRES but he doesn't talk. God has no vocal chords!

IF GOD HAS NO BODY, and accompanying senses, as we do, how does he know things as we do? He doesn't!

Good stuff. John has, literally, thousands more of these "daily miscellanies."

A few weeks before I submitted this memoir to the printer, I received John's annual Christmas letter to his many relatives and few friends. He wrote: "The high of our year was reached on May 5th when I walked Krista down the aisle of St. Patrick's Church in center city Philadelphia for her marriage…Krista was beautiful as was the weather. I lost my composure halfway down the aisle. Everyone thought I was overcome by the emotion of the moment when in fact the sobs were brought on by the bill I'd just gotten for the Union League reception." I hope John and I can continue and even strengthen our new-found friendship. He is my only link to my high school days.

The final member of our clique was Ed Dailey: a genius, a rebel, an eccentric. Ed was volatile, highly animated. He never spoke; he orated. He never differed with you, he debated you, he harangued you. He was an atheist, a communist in high school, who debated and embarrassed his teachers in the classroom. He was also physically strong, as he proved one lunch period when he did ten one-handed pushups. He made the football team, but a knee injury prevented him from playing. Behind his tough, gruff exterior, he was a good, kind person and likeable. He won all kinds of scholarships and elected to go to Johns Hopkins University on a full four-year academic scholarship, where, I heard, he neglected his physical appearance and his studies and dropped out of school during his freshman year, never to be heard of or seen since. Gene, the private investigator, said he was going to search for him but he never did. The last I heard, years ago, he was driving a taxi in Philadelphia. I doubt if Ed is alive today. It seemed he was ready for a heart attack during his high school days.

68

Our Oblate teachers in high school knew when a new big band came to the Earle Theater in central Philadelphia: about a third of the class would be missing to catch the Monday matinee performance. When the teacher called the roll and a missing boy's name was called, somebody would call out "Earle" instead of "absent." I skipped school several times, but I usually went to the Earle for the Saturday matinee. I saw all the great big bands and vocalists of the 40s: The Dorsey brothers, Kay Kyser, Glenn Miller, Artie Shaw, Woody Herman, Harry James, etc. I heard Frank Sinatra when he was a skinny kid singing with Tommy Dorsey's band when the swoon age began.

Of course, we were not allowed to smoke in school at North Catholic nor were we allowed to smoke within a two-block radius of school property, which included the El station. Some fellows would try to sneak a cigarette at the far end of the field during lunch, but I swear somebody must have been using a telescope or binoculars because they often were picked out of line on our way into the school from lunch and given a demerit, which meant staying after school in the Jug. Fr. John Lynch, the lunch period proctor, certainly couldn't spot them with the naked eye. He couldn't see ten feet ahead. And that's a fact, as I learned when I lived with him in the Oblate Novitiate a few years later.

I thought Northeast Catholic was an excellent high school, considering the circumstances: an enrollment of 4,000 tough boys from tough, lower-medium income neighborhoods in an overcrowded school. Our classes were packed with 50 or more students. In a number of classes, students used the teachers' desk as their own. Others sat on the windowsills. We were constantly borrowing desks from nearby classrooms. Today, the school is on the verge of closing because of shrinking enrollment. The faculty house next to the school where I lived as a seminarian and, later, as a newly ordained priest, along with about 60 other priests, now sits empty.

The chief means of maintaining discipline was the demerit slip. Five demerits and you were suspended from attending classes. The only way to be reinstated was to have one of your parents come to see the principal. A demerit slip was a pass to JUG (Justice Under God), a detention room in the basement next to Room Five, the lavatory, where you sat for an hour in total silence with your hands folded on the desk in front of you.

Guards also helped with the discipline. They were students who were empowered by the administration to help maintain discipline. They wore distinctive red arm bands with NC emblazoned on them. To man their stations in the school to regulate traffic in the corridors and stairways, they left class five minutes early and returned to the next class five minutes late. They posted themselves about every 10 yards down the hundred yard, three storied corridors and at the two stairways at each end of the school. The students had to stay to the right of the guards and they were not allowed to cross over until the end of the corridor even if no student was coming in the opposite direction. The students had to walk up the up stairway only, even if no student was coming up the upstairs. This type of traffic control was necessary in a school of 4,000 students built for 3,000.

First Mass evening reception in Mom's home on Mercer St., June 18, 1957. Fr. George Godley, my former high school bowling coach on the left. My next older brother Walt on the right.

On Tuesdays, those who won a letter for making a sport or engaging in a school activity were allowed to wear the red school sweaters displaying the letter won for a sport or a school activity. On Mondays, freshmen were awarded numerals of the year they were to graduate. I won a numeral my first year but I never displayed it. My three remaining years, I displayed my bowling letter regularly. It may not have been a major sport letter, but I was proud of it.

We had Pep Rallies in the gym before important games. Half the school population was crammed into the basketball gym, all hollering, screaming, stamping their feet—pure bedlam—until Fr. Knobby Walsh (He looked like Knobby, the manager of the cartoon character, Joe Palooka, the boxer.), the disciplinarian, entered the gym and glared at us. Total silence prevailed thereafter. He was a master of crowd-control, better than Hitler ever was.

We had study halls in the auditorium. About 500 students occupied every other seat. In my sophomore year, Fr. George Godley, a small Irishman with a high-pitched, shrill voice and our bowling coach, was the proctor of the study hall. He would settle us down, quickly check the roll from a master chart, then leave, probably for a cigarette in the faculty room across the hall from the back of the auditorium. After about ten minutes, the students noticing that no one was watching them began to talk. From out of the back of the auditorium a piercing voice could be heard shouting, "Chrzanowski, stop your talking, or you'll go to Jug." But I was studying or writing with my head down—not talking. This happened three straight study classes. Finally, I found the courage to ask Fr. Godley on our way downtown to a bowling match. "Father, how come you always call out my name for talking when I'm probably the only kid not talking in study hall?" "Ed," he said, "your name is the only name I know in that study hall. If I call you by name, they all think I know all of them by name and they shut up for fear of getting a demerit."

A few years later as a seminarian with a year of novitiate and two years of college behind me, I found myself in the same situation as Fr. Godley. I was placed in charge of 500 students in the auditorium study hall. I never had to use Fr. Godley's tactic because I never dared leave the auditorium for a cigarette. I watched all of them intently. I knew one false move, one lapse on my part there would be pandemonium in that auditorium. It was sheer mental intensity, concentration and vigilance on my part that kept those 500 kids in line. I dreaded that one hour out of the week. I couldn't sleep the night before and I was drained for the rest of the day afterwards. But I kept order in that study hall.

We also had weekly Mass in the auditorium. I recall our freshman section was assigned to a place in the back of the balcony. I was scandalized when I saw nearby seniors eating their lunch during Mass and then receiving Holy Communion a few minutes later at the time when we were to fast from food and drink from midnight if we were to receive Holy Communion.

We had some great athletes at North Catholic during my time. Tom Kelleher was an outstanding end both on offense and defense. He went on to Holy Cross College on a football scholarship and then had a long career as a referee for the National Football League.

Bob Montgomery was a great running halfback who entered the priesthood for the Washington, D.C., diocese and became a monsignor. I noticed in our alumni newspaper that he died recently. Johnny Idzik was a quarterback who could pass and run. He received a football scholarship to Canisius College, a Jesuit college in nearby Buffalo where he starred for four years and later went on to coach football on the college and professional levels for many years. Howie Willis was also in the backfield with Johnny Idzik. They looked like twins. They were blond, good-looking, about the same height and weight, about 180 pounds and 5' 10". They had the same running and passing style and Howie also went to Canisius. He finished his schooling, but his football career was cut short in his sophomore year because of a knee injury. Joe Gould, a classmate, was a great guard. He was built close to the ground like a guard should be: 5'6", 220 pounds. I recall his catching in the closing seconds of the game a tipped pass for an interception and rumbling 90 yards for a touchdown that won the game for us. I was disappointed I didn't see Joe at our 50th reunion four years ago.

We had some great basketball players during my time at North Catholic. Larry Sullivan was a fiery player who charged the basket with reckless abandon. He was the first player I ever saw who drove to the basket and in midair laid the ball up to the basket underhanded. Larry was from Port Richmond, a member of the Irish church, the Nativity of the Blessed Virgin Mary, just three blocks from our Polish church, St. Adalbert's. Larry was frequently in trouble in and out of school. He never went to college because of poor grades. Bernie O'Toole, a teammate of Sullivan, who also learned his basketball at Nativity's small gym, was a classy ball handler, who often fed the ball to Larry Sullivan on his drives to the basket. Larry was Mr. Inside and Bernie was Mr. Outside with his long two-handed set shots from the outside. Tommy Huckel, a classmate of ours, from St. Anne's on the perimeter of Port Richmond on Lehigh Avenue, was a great two-handed set shooter and ball handler. He set the Catholic league record for the highest points scored in an individual game—46.

Back then, everybody shot a basketball from the outside two-handed and with both feet on the ground. It wasn't until a few years later, that Joe Fulks of the Philadelphia Warriors, as they were then known, revolutionized the game of basketball by introducing the one-handed jump shot. Fulks was shortly followed by Paul Arizin from Villanova and Tom Gola from LaSalle, two local college greats, who went on to play for the Warriors.

I recall watching Tom Gola when he played for LaSalle High School. I was a seminarian living with about ten priests and five other seminarians in a three-story double home in downtown Philadelphia, at 13th and Pine. We commuted every day to teach at North Catholic, about a half-hour ride by car. We seminarians got special permission from Fr. Ward, our superior, to watch the great Tom Gola play against North Catholic in a night game. Back then, rarely were we seminarians allowed out at night, even to watch our school play basketball. I was the oldest of the seminarians at the time so I was put in charge. We were told emphatically by Fr. Ward to be back by 10 o'clock. The game went into overtime. It was 9:30. The other seminarians looked at me. I said, "Let's stay. Fr. Ward will understand." We stayed for the overtime period, and we won the game. Fr. Ward did not understand. We arrived back home about 10:30 and before I had time to explain about the overtime, he scolded me terribly. "I told you specifically to be back no later than ten o'clock." "But, Father…" "No buts about it. You violated an obedience. Don't ever ask me to go out at night again, now get to bed." We never did ask him again.

We did see Tom Gola play again on a Sunday afternoon in our gym at North Catholic. Tom was hot that day. He was making all kinds of shots until about half way through the fourth period, a buzz was going on among the crowd. Tom was threatening to beat Tommy Huckle's record of 46 points in a single game. Gola had 38 points with three minutes to play. Phil

Looby, our coach, to preserve Tommy Huckle's record told the team not to worry about the outcome of the game, it was really lost already, but to freeze the ball, to keep the ball away from Tom Gola. Back then, there was no 24 second shot clock. Tom Gola, of course, knew he was close to the record. With time running out, he became a madman, a man possessed. For the last three minutes he was frantically chasing, almost single handedly, after the ball as it was being passed from one player to another. He deliberately fouled our player, got the rebound from the missed foul shot, ran down the full length of the court, and laid the ball up. He now had 40 points. He intercepted the in-bounds pass under his own basket, and laid up for another two points. He now had 42 points. Tom now had 4 fouls and couldn't foul again. We got the ball in bounds and froze the ball until time ran out. A disconsolate and upset Tom Gola left the floor for the locker room. Phil Looby was criticized for his tactic, and, I think, rightly so.

My oldest brother Joe attended Northeast Catholic High School for two years many years before I did until he was old enough to work where my father worked. He enjoyed reminiscing about those years especially when he had a few drinks in him. He told me how Fr. Greene, calling the role, "Amico, Andretti, Antonucci, Buglioni..." paused and remarked, "This class seems wop-sided." And when he came to Joe's name, scratched his head, and said, "I'll have to sneeze this name." He told me how he was embarrassed in religion class when he couldn't recite the Our Father and Hail Mary in English, and when he recited them in Polish the class laughed at him. He told me he was proud of fellow Poles, Joe "Bones" Konieczny, a star fullback on the football team and Al "Pretzels" Przesztelski for being selected as captain of the guards, a student organization that controlled traffic in the corridors and aided the school administration in other ways. But when Joe reached 16, Pop got him a job at the Kokies, the nickname for Koppers Koke Co., in

Bridesburg, which alleviated the financial situation at home considerably.

We had a senior trip to New York City near the end of our senior year. We all looked forward to it. For me and many others, it was our first trip to the Big Apple. About 800 seniors boarded a specially chartered train at North Philadelphia station at Broad and Glenwood Avenues. Many were looking forward to the trip because they heard they would be able to drink liquor in New York City. The five of us, John Murphy, John Collins, Gene Boyle, Ed Dailey, and I spent a quiet and enjoyable day in New York City. We went to Central Park, the zoo, several museums, and had lunch. We arrived at the train terminal 7:00 P.M. Departure was at 8:00. The 800 mostly drunken rowdy students took over the terminal. They sang our Alma Mater song, they shouted our pep rally cheers, "Fablio N. Fablio C. E niko dimo N. E niko dimo C, etc." The three seminarians acting as proctors for the excursion stood by silently, sullenly, unable to do anything about the shameful display. We boarded the train and halfway home on the three-hour ride, all mayhem broke out.

Students attacked and stole the concessionaire's goods; they kicked out windows, urinated wherever. The three seminarians watched all this helplessly.

The following day we wondered what the response would be from the administration. What punishment would be meted out? Nothing. Just the simple, terse announcement by Fr. Ed Smith, the principal, over the public address system: "There will no longer be any senior trips." It was not a nice way to finish our high school days.

Nor is it a nice way to finish this memoir. A few months later from that same train station at Broad and Glenwood Avenues, I boarded a train, not to New York City, but in an opposite direction to the south, to Wilmington, Delaware, where a bus awaited to take us 30 candidates for the priesthood as Oblates of St. Francis de Sales an additional 25 miles across the countryside of Maryland to Childs, the site of the novitiate where every new candidate had to spend the first 15 months of his long quest to the priesthood.

The End

About the Author

Ed Chrzanowski, the youngest of four sons, was born in 1929 in a tough, poor Polish neighborhood in Northeast Philadelphia, known as Port Richmond. At age 18, he entered the seminary. In 1957, he was ordained a priest of the Oblates of St. Francis de Sales. After teaching high school in Philadelphia, Niagara Falls, and Toledo, he left the priesthood in 1977 and married in 1980. He settled in Lockport, NY, about twenty miles from Buffalo and Niagara Falls. Since then he has taught high school, college, at Attica State Prison, sold real estate, insurance, and various other items. He wrote for two local dailies, *The Niagara Gazette* and *The Buffalo News.* At present, he works as a Legal Researcher for the *Buffalo Law Journal,* a sister publication of *Business First,* and has his own resume writing business.